BROKEN

BROKEN

How the Global Pandemic Uncovered a Nursing Home System in Need of Repair and the Heroic Staff Fighting for Change

DR. BUFFY LLOYD-KREJCI

BROKEN
How the Global Pandemic Uncovered a Nursing Home System in Need of Repair and the Heroic Staff Fighting for Change

ISBN 978-1-5445-2835-9 *Hardcover*
978-1-5445-2836-6 *Paperback*
978-1-5445-2837-3 *Ebook*

To my beloved Brian for giving me the courage to be brave when faced with fear and to boldly speak for those that can't. I love you.

CONTENTS

FOREWORD

by Peter P. Patterson, M.D.,
Glencroft Center for Modern Aging, Glendale, Arizona

In late December 2019, cases of "Wuhan pneumonia" in China were reported to the Centers for Disease Control and Prevention (CDC) in Atlanta, Georgia, and major academic centers in the United States. On January 19, 2020, a thirty-two-year-old man traveled from Wuhan to his home in Snohomish County, Washington. He developed symptoms, was diagnosed with pneumonia, and hospitalized. He recovered ten days later. On February 28, 2020, a case of the "Wuhan pneumonia," now known as "Coronavirus disease 2019" (COVID-19), was identified in a female resident of a long-term care (LTC) facility in King County, Washington. Subsequent epidemiologic investigation identified eighty-one residents, thirty-four staff members, and fourteen visitors associated with that facility as having COVID-19. Of those 129 people, thirty-eight died, and Seattle became the epicenter for the first United States outbreak of COVID-19 in LTC facilities. Many such outbreaks followed as COVID-19 spread rapidly across the United States.

The COVID-19 pandemic caught everyone unaware. At first, no one knew how easily the virus transmitted, and, more importantly, how much viral spread could occur among asymptomatic residents and staff. As the nursing home industry became more knowledgeable, caregiving infection control practices had to change from week-to-week, even day-to-day. LTC facilities everywhere struggled to find supplies of personal protective equipment (PPE): masks, gowns, and face shields. With insufficient protection, doctors, nurses, and other caregiving staff contracted COVID-19. Many lost their lives. For caregivers, the pandemic became a national tragedy mixed with individual heroism.

Amid a rising chorus of public outrage, surveyors from federal and state regulatory agencies began an urgent campaign to inspect LTC facilities that had reported outbreaks. Surveyors could quickly identify infection control practices that were below the latest standard of care, even though those same practices may have been the proper procedures only a few weeks earlier. Under the strict regulatory process, surveyors could not offer helpful suggestions to surveyed facilities, only formal citations and fines. Their only tool was the hammer of fault-finding. Therefore, deficient care practices looked like nails that needed pounding. And pound away they did, issuing a stream of citations and fines to surveyed facilities that then had to take time away from care to respond with formal plans of correction. This cruel combination of regulatory burden on top of the pandemic burden created widespread stress and burnout in facility administration and staff.

Dr. Buffy Lloyd-Krejci did part of her epidemiological training at the CDC and was well-known to the LTC community. Her small consulting firm was frequently retained to assist facilities with their infection prevention and control programs. Called to action, Dr. Buffy quickly threw herself into the huge task of working with administrators and staff at LTC facilities across the United States.

FOREWORD

What began as a journal to cope with overwhelming feelings quickly turned into a record of personal stories and research around the circumstances. *BROKEN: How the Global Pandemic Uncovered a Nursing Home System in Need of Repair and the Heroic Staff Fighting for Change* is a clarion call to every person in the United States who has, or who will have, a beloved family member or elder friend living in a nursing home, or a family member needing transitional care between a hospital stay and a return to home.

This book exposes many uncomfortable truths about the pandemic response and our LTC system. But light on these dark issues is the best catalyst for needed positive change. Dr. Lloyd-Krejci shines a light on those truths and invites readers to see for themselves the true sources of problems in the delivery of care for this vulnerable population. From there, anyone—resident or advocate, caregiver, administrator, policymaker, or legislator—can follow Dr. Lloyd-Krejci's lead and choose how they might participate in restoring the integrity of the post-acute care system.

How a society conducts itself in a disaster such as a pandemic is a measure of its overall health and well-being. Dr. Lloyd-Krejci is calling us to share her commitment to creating the needed political alliances and high-level agreements between all of us who are stakeholders in this great task of caring for our vulnerable community members. Awakening to this call is crucial to the future of our communities of caregivers, healers, and especially our elders.

INTRODUCTION

"I'll never go into a nursing home."

Most of us have said this, and many of us believe it. But the truth is that staying out of a care facility simply may not be an option, once we reach an age or circumstance that incapacitates us.

If you have a loved one in the care of a nursing home, you already know this. But you may not know the true nature of the environment where your family member now lives, or what you can do to advocate change—not only for your loved one, but for those who follow. What will it take for Americans to feel comfortable with long-term care?

It's a fair question. In the United States, nearly sixteen thousand nursing homes provide care to over four million people every year.[1] As the baby boomer generation (those born between 1946 through 1964) ages, more of us will require long-term care services. In fact, it is estimated that eighty-eight million Americans will need long-term care services in 2050; this is an 84 percent increase from the forty-eight million that required services in 2015.[2]

Before the COVID-19 pandemic, long-term care facilities, commonly known as nursing homes, did not have a strong focus on infection control practices. It was no surprise that the Centers for Disease Control and Prevention (CDC) estimated that nearly three million severe infections led to 380,000 deaths each year.[3] That's more than a thousand deaths per day. While these statistics are scary, the most maddening aspect of these numbers is the estimated percentage of preventable infections. Conservative estimates say 40 percent, while some suggest up to 70 percent of infections, are preventable. Even on the low end, *we are talking about saving four hundred lives every day.*[4] The consequences of not having infection control as a priority is dire.

These numbers and other equally startling information felt to me like a personal call to action. In the spring of 2018, I left my cushy corporate job with its health insurance and 401(k) and dedicated myself full-time to bringing awareness of this preventable problem. I reached out to hundreds of nursing homes, corporate leaders, and federal decision-makers including the Centers for Medicare and Medicaid Services (CMS), the primary payer and regulatory licensing agency for long-term care services, and told them, "There's a problem here, and I can help you with it."

It felt as though we were on the Titanic—the iceberg, straight ahead—and few cared what I had to say. Thinking perhaps that spreading the message alone was the problem, my husband quit his job and joined me in my outreach effort. Believing in our cause so deeply and recognizing the magnitude of the problem, we innocently thought that facilities would jump to get on board as long as we arrived with a solution to solving the problem of infection control.

It turned out we were mistaken. After a year of making hundreds of phone calls, sending thousands of emails, conducting dozens of free webinars, and presenting at conferences across the country, only seven nursing homes hired us to help them improve their infection control program. The government response wasn't much better. I presented a detailed plan to the long-term care CMS team on how to reduce resident harms and deaths due to infectious diseases with no follow-up; no action steps were taken to move forward with the plan.

So why do I keep going? Why bring this issue forward into 2022 and beyond? The time is long past due to provide safe and effective care to our long-term care residents and a safe environment for the dedicated staff. As an expert in long-term care infection prevention and control, I have supported hundreds of nursing homes across the country and have witnessed the devasting consequences of COVID-19.

The stories have all been the same: lack of support, lack of understanding, and a governmental approach that includes a system of bullying, fines, and punishment that dictate every change in this healthcare setting. Representatives of Doctors Without Borders, nursing home administrators, academic researchers, national and international advocacy groups, state licensing agencies, healthcare workers, and patients all have a different story to tell.

Given the punitive regulatory environment of this industry, I have changed many of the names of the individuals in these pages to protect their identities. But you'll hear them describe the challenges in nursing homes prior to the COVID-19 pandemic, alongside my own personal experience with grandparents who lived out their final days in a nursing home. I'll describe how academic researchers have published data for years about the infection control problems in nursing homes and the interventions that began prior to the pandemic.

I'll also describe the early response from nursing homes to COVID-19 and how the federal government chose to respond to nursing homes with a punitive strategy, rather than one that was collaborative and supportive.

Finally, I'll describe how we can use this dark season to transform the long-term care industry into a supportive healthcare system that provides safer, more reliable care for our loved ones.

If you have a loved one now in the care of a nursing or rehabilitation home, this book will equip you to understand the true nature of that environment and what you can do to advocate change when necessary. Your actions will have a lasting impact! What will it take for us as citizens and community members to feel comfortable with long-term care? We should not have to cringe and say, "I'll never go into a nursing home," because that may not be the reality.

Now is the time to create change and to have our voices heard. Together, we can assist in shifting punitive strategies of control to a culture of collaboration and support, a culture that provides the best opportunity to give residents the care they deserve—and the working conditions expert caregivers are worthy of receiving.

CHAPTER 1

A HOUSE ON FIRE

"It isn't that they can't see the solution. It's that they can't see the problem. They can't see the problem if they are looking in the wrong place. They can't see the problem if they have blinders on— for 'none are so blind as those that will not see.'"

—Gilbert K. Chesterton

November 25, 2018, Baltimore, MD

My heart is racing.

I can't get to my computer fast enough. I need to ring an alarm bell; let government officials—the world!—know about the atrocities I've discovered in a local nursing home. I know that, once the right people know what's going on, they'll race to remedy the situation and help the facility.

I'm here in Baltimore as a consultant for a public health organization. Concerned about the care her ninety-four-year-old aunt Nannie was receiving, Crystal, the organization's administrative assistant has asked me to visit the Patuxent Health and Rehabilitation Center, where Nannie lives. Crystal knew of my expertise in infection prevention and control (IPC) in nursing homes and trusted my opinion of her aunt's current care home.

We'd headed for the nursing home on a cold autumn day—something I, a longtime Phoenix resident, wasn't accustomed to. We planned to attend a family council meeting, a perfect opportunity to visit and hear the concerns of family members of the facility's residents. We arrived after a forty-five-minute drive; it was after-hours, but the doors were still open for the meeting.

The smell of urine smacked me in the face as soon as I walked in the door.

Twenty or thirty years ago, a person might have expected this rank odor in any nursing home, but it's much less common today. I introduced myself to a tall blonde seated at the reception desk, who surprised me with the news that she was the nursing home's administrator.

Didn't she notice the smell?

I explained I was there to support my friend Crystal, that I was an infection control expert, and would participate in the meeting. As I handed her my card, I assumed she'd feel delighted to take advantage of my knowledge. I really thought she would welcome outside support. Little did I know!

The meeting room was full. Among those there to represent their loved ones was Crystal's ninety-two-year-old mother Violet, seated in a wheelchair. She traveled across town on two buses every other day to visit her ninety-four-year-old sister "Nannie."

Crystal explained to the group that I was there to listen, learn, and hopefully help. The meeting started with a lot of legal jargon about recent state legislative actions, but I snapped to full attention when talk turned to the recent outbreak of scabies, a highly contagious infection that causes itching from mites that live beneath the skin. The council members, suspecting a cover-up, complained that this "five-star" facility hadn't notified the families of this outbreak. They argued that it was the mother of a resident and the family council president, Twila Bridges, who'd contacted the state's Office of Health Care Quality (OHCQ) and reported an urgent need for help. It took a patient advocate to ensure that every resident was treated for the scabies. Sadly, for one resident, it was too late. He'd scratched himself badly enough that his skin became infected. He developed sepsis (a bloodstream infection) and died. I sat in shock as I heard the description of this tragedy about a human life that could have easily been spared with the early identification and treatment of the infection.

As the meeting continued, council members reported other potentially fatal infectious outbreaks such as *Klebsiella pneumonia*, *Clostridioides difficile*, and influenza. One daughter told of how her mother continued to get urinary tract infections (UTIs). Because she was also immunocompromised, the woman worried that the condition would lead to sepsis and cause her mother's death.

I knew the dangers of sepsis, a life-threatening condition with an associated mortality rate of up to 41.1 percent. Sepsis secondary to a UTI accounts for nearly 25 percent of all sepsis cases. The urinary tract is the second most common infection site, accounting for approximately 20 percent to 40 percent of all severe cases of sepsis in patients.[1] Given the high incidence and severity of sepsis, early recognition and appropriate management of UTIs play a vital role in preventing the disease progression to urosepsis.

I was frantically taking notes, trying not to miss one word. What could I do now? Who could help them? The family members mentioned they'd already contacted their Ombudsman, appointed by the facility to record complaints, and even called on Maryland state senator Jim Rosapepe for help (he'd eventually assist in making changes). The families had taken these actions yet had been largely ignored until this point.

Crystal and I needed to leave the meeting to visit Nannie while she was still awake. As we left, I made a sincere promise to the group to do everything I could to help. The frustration in one family member's outburst startled me.

"That's what they all say! You're not going to help. Nobody ever helps!"

Others stepped in to quiet her, to keep her from offending me, but I felt her pain. Her cries had gone unanswered. To her, I was just another voice promising to make a change. I let her vent. When she was done, I reassured her that I'd recently quit my job expressly to assist in solving this problem. I knew she didn't believe me. Why would she? So far, no one had supported her. I left the meeting feeling heartbroken.

Walking down the hall beside Crystal, I noticed there were no hand sanitizing dispensers in the hallway. How did anyone practice hand hygiene? There were none in Nannie's room, either. Two nurses came in to provide care to Nannie's roommate, neither washed their hands before or after providing care.

"They never do," Crystal told me. There was a sink in the restroom—not a suitable place to practice consistent hand hygiene—but it went unused. No wonder these infectious outbreaks were occurring; they weren't implementing basic infection-control practices. How was the nursing home staff passing over something so fundamental?

I made an instant connection with Nannie, a strong, feisty African American woman. She was in continual pain, though; the arthritis in her hip was unbearable. Crystal and I gave her a back and hip rub to ease the pain. Crystal told her that I was there "to help."

Nannie looked at me with conviction and said, "Good. We need it." She then offered me a piece of her much-valued bubble gum, a simple yet meaningful gesture, that solidified our new friendship.

Back in my hotel room, I opened my laptop. *I will sound the alarm*, I thought as I began an email to the leaders of the Centers for Medicare and Medicaid Services (CMS). I described the outbreaks at Nannie's facility, the lack of help from the state and other advocates. I pled with them to make this a priority, told them I was willing to fight this battle one nursing home at a time. With their help, their influence, their power, I typed, we could make an immense difference and decrease the risk of harm and death due to infections. Based on my studies, I explained, this situation was not an isolated event. It was a countrywide, systemic issue.

Exhausted, I crawled into bed. *There*, I thought as I drifted into a fitful sleep. *I've started the ball rolling. Once the powers that be are aware of what I've seen tonight, they'll jump in and we'll start making a difference.*

I had no way of knowing how mistaken I was.

CHAPTER 2

FROM APARTMENT TO *HOME*

"We cannot turn the clock back, nor can we undo the harm caused, but we have the power to determine the future and to ensure that what has happened never happens again."

—Paul Kagame

Four long days later, I receive a reply to my email from the CMS leaders. The Director of Beneficiary Health Improvement and Safety writes to say the first step is to have "patients and their family members contact their BFCC-QIO when they have quality of care concerns and complaints about nursing homes. When appropriate, we make any needed referral to state or federal survey agencies."

I'm appalled to receive such a generic response. The Beneficiary and Family-Centered Care Quality Improvement Organizations (BFCC-QIOs) assist Medicare recipients with high-quality care. He must not have understood my email. The family council had already contacted the BFCC-QIO, the state, and their state senator. I'm sure the way I felt brushed aside is similar to how family members, such as those in the family council meeting, have felt all along.

Little did this CMS leadership team and everyone who'd served before them know, this plea would serve as an early warning sign of what was to come just eighteen months later, in the form of a deadly virus that would ravage the world, hitting nursing homes the hardest and claiming hundreds of thousands of lives.

I was grateful my grandparents, whom I'd affectionately called Mee Mee and Dee Dee, weren't here to witness this.

They'd had my mother late in life, at ages forty-three and forty-five, so by the time I was born they were nearly seventy years old. Mee Mee and Dee Dee had lived in their tiny one-bedroom apartment on University Drive in Mesa, Arizona, for my entire life. The apartment complex was a small pink building with beautiful rose bushes all along the outside, right underneath their windows. Going to visit Mee Mee and Dee Dee is a favorite childhood memory of mine. I loved pulling up to their apartment, where we were welcomed by the white stone mama duck and her ducklings. Dee Dee's bright yellow 1970s Chevy Malibu was parked in the carport with a yellow lovebird hanging from the rearview mirror.

My family lived about ninety miles away from Mee Mee and Dee Dee in a small country town in northern Arizona. Back then, there was only a single-lane highway between our house and theirs. If there were any slow-moving vehicles, it could take almost two hours to get there. Our visits didn't happen as often as I would have liked, so I soaked up the time with them while I had it. Dee Dee was a strong, solid man of German descent. He was handsome at six feet tall, with a sturdy frame, jet-black hair, and tattoos that covered both arms. I'd sit on his lap and he would tell me the story of how a seventeen-year-old getting tattoos in 1922 was an incredibly rebellious act. He described the day he got the first set of them, two on each arm, a Kewpie doll and nurse on one, a heart with an arrow and rose on the other. He would explain how he was doing his chores outside, and unable to bear the heat, took off his long sleeve shirt, revealing his indiscretion. He recounted the whooping he received from his father as a result.

He told me that the tattoo on the top of his left arm, the Kewpie doll, was me.

When I was seventeen years old, I moved to Mesa, Arizona, not far from where Mee Mee and Dee Dee lived. By this time, both of them were in their late eighties and slowly declining. Daily activities like getting groceries and cooking meals were becoming more challenging. When my mother would discuss moving them into a nursing home for the additional support, they would dismiss the notion immediately. As a family, we tried getting them to at least accept food services from Meals on Wheels, but even this was refused. As a result, I would bring them seven days' worth of meals every Sunday—simple meals like prepared lasagna or Hamburger Helper. One day, I went to retrieve a pan from their oven and discovered they were using this appliance for storage, meaning they were eating the meals cold (they didn't own a microwave, by choice).

When I was nineteen years old, I got the call that Dee Dee had fallen on the sidewalk, broke his hip, and needed immediate surgery. The hip replacement surgery went well, but he was going to need several weeks to rehabilitate. Once he was medically cleared from the hospital, he was transferred to a skilled nursing facility (SNF), also known as a nursing home or rehabilitation center.

After a few weeks, it became clear that Dee Dee would not be well enough to ever return to their apartment again. He needed round-the-clock support; returning home was not a viable option. The news was not surprising to me, having witnessed his gradual decline. I was simultaneously sad and relieved.

Shortly after that, our family was able to convince Mee Mee to move into the same facility so she could also receive care and spend time with her husband. Mee Mee and Dee Dee lived in separate rooms where they had a roommate of the same sex. This was the most affordable option for them at one hundred dollars per day, which would be paid with their life savings. My family had hoped they could stay in the same room together, but at least Mee Mee could shuffle down the hall to see him every day. Mee Mee and Dee Dee never seemed to return to their normal selves once they entered the facility. I believe relinquishing their freedom and having others take care of them ate away at their pride, and it soon seemed like they'd given up on life.

I visited them every week and remember the smell distinctly: urine with a hint of Old Spice permeated a "place like this." Mee Mee and Dee Dee were always happy to have Katie, my two-year-old daughter, and me visit. Dee Dee's face would always light up when he saw Katie. Our visits were brief but meaningful.

On February 4, 1994, on a Sunday afternoon after church, my family, including my husband, Katie, and two-month-old daughter Chelsey went to visit. It was Dee Dee's ninetieth birthday. From the time I could remember, Dee Dee always told me that he would live to ninety. Oddly, I find myself thinking the same thing about my own life. Dee Dee was in a wheelchair in the hallway next to the nursing station. He had lost some weight and looked smaller in stature, but I knew that strong, proud man was still there. When I introduced him to his new great-granddaughter, Chelsey, he smiled and said, "She's cute."

We didn't stay too long, as Dee Dee looked tired. I kissed him goodbye and told him I loved him.

At two in the morning, I received a phone call from the nursing home that Dee Dee had passed away, sound asleep in his bed, just as he'd predicted. The nursing staff asked me to come down to the facility to break the news to Mee Mee. I knew that she, having spent forty-six years with Dee Dee, would be devastated.

At the facility, Mee Mee was still asleep. I touched her arm and whispered her name. She slowly opened her eyes, confused. I didn't know how to get the words out.

"What? What?" she asked me.

"It's Dee Dee...he's passed on."

She looked at me, unable to comprehend the words I'd just said.

"He's gone," I repeated.

"No...no..." her voice trembled. "It can't be."

The nurse and I got Mee Mee up and helped her to Dee Dee's room, where she sat in a chair next to him, holding his hand and quietly sobbing. I'll never forget the day I lost my gentle giant.

Mee Mee spent the next two years of her life in a nursing home. I still went every week to visit, sometimes bringing a third great-granddaughter, Meagan, for her to enjoy. One day I came to visit Mee Mee without the babies. After a hectic day, I wanted to go and see her alone. Boy, was that a mistake. She was so mad that she wouldn't even look at me.

"Don't ever come here without those babies!" she told me. She would have nothing to do with me for the rest of the very short visit. Needless to say, I never made that mistake again.

On January 3, 1998, Mee Mee took her last breath, also at the age of ninety. She had had a stroke a week earlier, and this was her final goodbye. The nurses called to tell me she was having labored breathing and the end was near. I was able to sit next to her bed and hold her hand as she gently slipped from this world into the next. It was an intense moment for me as a twenty-year-old young lady, my first encounter with someone as they passed away. My heart was heavy with grief. I remember looking out her bedroom window and seeing a beautiful ray of sunlight shining down. I felt instant comfort knowing that she was with Dee Dee again. I'll always be grateful for the experience of helping my beloved grandparents leave this earth with dignity and grace. Little did I know, this experience would guide me in my future work, improving the safety and care of residents of nursing homes.

CHAPTER 3

THE INVISIBLE ENEMY

"The unseen enemy is always the most fearsome."
—George RR Martin

In early January 2020, I heard rumblings of a deadly virus circulating in Wuhan, China. I didn't give it too much thought, given the US was in the middle of influenza season, and I was trying to prevent outbreaks from occurring in the nursing homes I was working with in Arizona. I was frustrated this story was gaining so much media attention, knowing that hundreds of thousands of residents die every year in nursing homes from serious infections without any commentary or coverage.

Fast forward to March 2021. By then, more than 1.4 million residents and long-term care employees had contracted coronavirus and more than 178,000 had died, making up 34 to 40 percent of all United States deaths from COVID-19.[1]

Many died isolated and alone, shut away from their loved ones, unable to sit with them, hold their hand, and tell them they love them as they took their last breath.

This loss, and the collective grief, panic, and fear appended to it, is now branded as an epic, historical event, prompting numerous questions: How did this happen? Where did we go wrong? When those questions are answered later, arrogance and negligence will bubble to the surface; fingers will be pointed. Culpability will shift. We'll discover that industry leaders knew about the shortcuts and the problems lying beneath the surface in nursing homes, that dozens of scientific studies pointed to high infection rates in nursing homes prior to the COVID-19 pandemic.

Answering the question of how this happened is vital to ensure this doesn't happen again. This is what keeps me up at night. Will we let history repeat itself—or not?

There are nearly sixteen thousand CMS-certified nursing homes in the United States. In 2016, there were 1,347,600 residents in nursing homes.[2]

That's more than a million of our mothers, fathers, sisters, children, aunts, uncles, friends, and neighbors living in a congregate setting away from their loved ones. In all cases, these "residents," otherwise known as "patients," are either unable to or have a limited capacity to care for themselves. (This doesn't include those living in assisted- or independent-living facilities.)

There are many different types of care offered in nursing homes. Many residents will receive short-term care or rehabilitation, usually in fewer than one hundred days. It's common for an individual of any age to receive medical care and treatment that's no longer appropriate in an acute-care hospital. This is why Dee Dee went into the nursing home: a short rehabilitation stay. There are others who require long-term care beyond one hundred days, and they'll probably die in the facility.

Long-term care is reserved for residents with dementia or the inability to physically care for themselves any longer. Dee Dee and ultimately Mee Mee became long-term care residents when it was determined by their medical provider that it was simply too dangerous for them to live on their own anymore. Making a choice to have your loved one enter a nursing home for long-term care is never easy and weighs heavily on those who've had to participate in the decision.

In American culture, this is how we've decided our elderly and disabled will live out their days. But it's not true for many cultures. Lanie, a nursing home administrator from Lee Summit, Missouri, came to the US in 1991 from the Philippines with her H1 Visa, which enabled her as an immigrant to gain employment here as a nurse.

Lanie was shocked to learn how Americans treat our elders at the end of their lives. In her culture, they "take care of their own," in part because of a tradition of multi-generational living. When a young couple gets married, they live with their parents, and as their children marry, they do the same. When grandma is old and frail, there are plenty of family members there to care for her.

It took Lanie some time to acclimate to the elderly and demented living away from family, and she took it upon herself to care for residents as if they were her own relations. This is, in part, why she has had a successful career in the industry for over twenty-five years.

For a nursing home to qualify as "certified," they must meet specific federal requirements under the Medicare and Medicaid programs, including implementing policies and practices of standards for quality of care, quality of life, and life safety requirements. In 1987, when the National Academy of Science's Institute of Medicine (IOM) reported a lack of quality care within the nursing home industry, Congress enacted legislative changes in an attempt to improve healthcare quality.[3]

This was much-needed reform, yet clearly only the beginning as the Government Accountability Office (GAO) continued to receive documented reports identifying residents who experienced serious harm in the trusted care of a nursing home. Perhaps this is the reason Mee Mee and Dee Dee fought so hard when the topic of moving permanently into a nursing home was brought up. The reputation surrounding nursing homes was poor, and for good reason.

In 1987, to combat the onslaught of reported complaints, the federal government issued a new rule requiring all certified nursing homes to hold quarterly quality meetings with a designated team—such as the medical director, administrator, and director of nursing—all working in and for the nursing home, to oversee any complaints or harm toward the residents. In addition, the government began evaluating the quality of care being delivered in facilities.[4]

When Mee Mee and Dee Dee were residents, phrases like *quality measures*, *quality meetings*, and *quality improvement* were only whispers in the conversation about change. I knew their facility smelled like urine, but wasn't that just the norm? Honestly, not knowing any better, I didn't know what I didn't know. The hospital had placed Dee Dee there. We, as a family, didn't select the facility where he would rehabilitate, live, and eventually die. There were few ways of knowing if a facility was even "good" or not. We didn't necessarily understand what to look for, and nobody offered us an explanation. I never once talked to a social worker or was a member of the care-planning team or heard of a family council meeting, which is today all very much integrated into a resident's care and admission.

In 2008, CMS implemented the five-star quality rating system, assigning value to health inspections, nurse staffing hours, and selected quality measures.[5] This system consists of fifteen physical and clinical criteria.[6] If a facility has five stars, then it's considered to deliver above-average quality care to residents. Conversely, a facility with only one star is considered below average in their delivery of care. When my beloved grandparents were assigned to a nursing home, I was simply grateful that they would have the help they needed and felt relieved knowing someone would look after them. I was naïve to the historical issues with nursing homes. Maybe I didn't really want to know or was too young to fully understand.

Fourteen years have passed since the five-star quality rating came into existence. There's a "caution" statement on the CMS website that indicates that there is "no rating system that can ultimately decide which nursing home is the best fit for an individual." The messaging goes on to explain to the consumer that they should "only use the data from the website along with other considerations such as location and cost when considering the placement of their loved one."[7] The bottom line is that there's no measuring process without flaw and, as you'll learn, CMS did not indicate whether a facility had more or less COVID-19 cases.

In 2010, the Patient Protection and Affordable Care Act adopted new policies requiring nursing homes to increase transparency and accountability regarding ownership, finances, staffing, and quality measures to evaluate the incidence of pressure sores, physical restraints, pain, loss of mobility, and other conditions associated with care.[8] This meant that nursing homes were required to report even more specific outcomes for the public and government entities to view and from which to make informed decisions.

It's interesting to note that none of the quality measures required the reporting of infectious diseases, thereby leaving consumers and the industry in the dark to the enormous problem lying under the surface. In quality improvement, we often say, "If you don't measure it, it doesn't get worked on." We can definitely say that this applied to infection prevention.

In 2009, the Office of Disease Prevention and Health Promotion (ODPHP), under the US Department of Health and Human Services, provided a national action plan to prevent healthcare-associated infections in acute care hospitals. In 2013, given the increased medical care services provided outside of the hospital setting, the action plan was expanded to include ambulatory surgical centers, end-stage renal disease facilities, and long-term care facilities.[9] Unfortunately, the steering committee chose to address infections in the long-term care setting as the final or "third" phase of the program even though early research from over a decade earlier estimated the number of infections in nursing homes was estimated to be 1.6 to 3.8 million in 16,700 US nursing homes, contributing to 150,000 hospitalizations and an annual cost of $673 million in additional healthcare costs.[10]

Wait, what?

That's nearly four million infections every year from one healthcare setting!

Note the word *estimated*. The report went on to acknowledge that the data was limited and only an estimate because it represented research studies in nursing homes that were more than ten years old. In addition, data that was pulled from even older research studies showed that there could be as many as 380,000 deaths in nursing homes every year.

From that information alone, I could write an entire book. However, prior to the COVID-19 pandemic, it's likely the world would not have cared. If the industry had taken this published data seriously, much could have been done. Nine years later, although some changes have been made, it's certainly not enough in an industry that operates well below evidence-based practices.

In actuality, the true burden of infections in nursing homes is still unknown because there's no standard of practice for reporting infections, known as "surveillance." To date, nursing homes are still not required to report their healthcare-associated infections to a national surveillance database, although there has been advancement toward this objective.

In 2015, I was working as a healthcare analyst for a Quality Improvement Network-Quality Improvement Organization (QIN-QIO), a program funded by the US Department of Health and Human Services. It's considered one of the largest federal programs dedicated to improving the quality of healthcare at the community level. I was responsible for analyzing hundreds of hospitals' healthcare-associated infection data reported to the QIN-QIO from five states. Hospitals participating in the program did so on a voluntary basis, with the knowledge that we'd provide technical support in helping them understand their data and set targeted, data-driven goals to reduce the incidence of HAIs such as Central-Line Associated Blood Stream Infection (CLABSI), Catheter-Associated Urinary Tract Infection (CAUTI), and *Clostrodioides difficile*, also known as C.-Diff.

I enjoyed working with the data and identifying opportunities to support hospitals, but I wasn't involved in actually working with the hospitals to implement change. So, when I was in a meeting with my small analytic team and was told we were going to start working on a national pilot project helping nursing homes report C.-Diff, the infectious disease that causes severe diarrhea, inflammation of the colon, and even death, I said, "Sign me up."

C.-Diff is known for its horrible smell and for causing volatile diarrhea. It is listed by the Centers for Disease Control and Prevention (CDC) as one of the most urgent antibiotic resistance threats in the United States. In 2019, there were 223,900 reported C.-Diff infections that led to nearly thirteen thousand deaths.[11] Risk factors for contracting C.-Diff include a current or recent hospital or healthcare stay and current or recent use of antibiotics. It can take months and even sometimes years to fully recover from this infection, and relapse is common. Nationally, nursing homes do not report this infection; therefore, the actual number of people contracting C.-Diff and the extent of the problem was and remains unknown.

This is one reason why the CDC and CMS began the national pilot project to begin reporting C.-Diff data into the Centers for Disease Control and Prevention's (CDC) National Healthcare Safety Network (NHSN), the nation's surveillance system for HAI reporting. There needed to be a clearer picture of the burden of C.-Diff to eventually combat it.

After an exciting meeting, I marched straight into my supervisor Catherine's office and declared that I wanted to work on the C.-Diff project. Though she was typically quiet and reserved, my declaration caught her off guard. The company didn't even have a final contract for the C.-Diff project. She probably wasn't used to staff so energetically volunteering for projects, which may be why she agreed.

I walked out of her office determined to work on helping nursing homes conduct surveillance and report this terrible disease. I wondered, *How could there be an infectious disease that causes so much harm not being recorded and fought?*

My prior experience analyzing infectious disease data gave me the confidence I knew could really make a difference. I had done so before, so why not again? In 2010, my peers and I worked on a Susceptible, Infected, Recovered (SIR) mathematical model that described the progression of the Human Papillomavirus (HPV), the most common sexually transmitted disease contributing to multiple health disparities and cancers in men and women. The research looked at targeted age groups of women to demonstrate the support for early immunization and screening programs to inform public health officials on the transmission of HPV and successfully showed the effectiveness of vaccination in both females and males. (Traditionally, only females were vaccinated for HPV.)

Later in 2013, I worked as a research affiliate with the Mayo Clinic as I completed my master's degree in biomedical informatics. I worked with a gastroenterologist analyzing enormous sets of healthcare data to evaluate patient outcomes for those with gastrointestinal bleeds. It was the most significant data set I had ever worked with, having over one hundred thousand data elements. I taught myself how to write code and statistically identify plausible correlations for various patient outcomes. These experiences told me that the start of a solution to C.-Diff lay within the data.

As indicated, the problem with my role with the QIO was that the departments were compartmentalized. Even though I had over a decade of healthcare experience and another five in research, I was limited to the analytics department writing SAS code, crunching the numbers and reports. Then these reports would go to the quality improvement team to actively work with the healthcare providers. This frustrated me, as I felt only a fraction of my skills were being utilized. After seven months in this role, in January of 2016, I decided to quit my job. I didn't want to be a code monkey and knew I could find a better way to make a greater impact in healthcare.

I was nervous the day I went into Catherine's office to put in my notice. I truly loved the work the QIO was doing, but I wasn't satisfied with my own work. I felt a bridge was needed between the analytics and the fieldwork. I explained all of this to Catherine and said, "Look, if I can work on the C.-Diff project and analyze data, that would be amazing."

"That's just not the way things work here," Catherine said. "But look, if you want to stay, I can find out if there's a different opportunity for you."

Within an hour, she called me on the phone.

"Michael A. wants to meet with you this afternoon." She said, "2:00 p.m. in his office."

Who was Michael A? I didn't ask for fear of looking foolish. I checked the company directory and saw that he was the vice president of the company. *Oh, shit! It must be good if he wants to meet me in person.*

Michael welcomed me with a warm smile and mentioned that the C.-Diff project was set to be awarded by CMS any day. His vision for the project was to have a designated task chair who would oversee the project for our four awarded states.

"We used to have this type of model in the past, but some states didn't like it," Michael said. "So, we did away with it. I want to do it again with this project."

Absolutely, excellent, you bet! I thought.

"I told Catherine I need you right away," he went on. "The sooner, the better. I told her you could give her two more weeks to get someone trained in your position, and then you'll be moved up."

I couldn't have been more thrilled. I completed my final two weeks in the analytics department and then moved up to the third floor. Unfortunately, my excitement soon changed to frustration as I quickly learned about the lack of communication within the leadership team. The conversation Michael and I had about me being the task chair never went beyond his office. In fact, for my first six months on the third floor, I knew that somebody named Jack was my supervisor and that he had me "chasing squirrels," as a good colleague of mine used to say. With seemingly no rhyme or reason to the tasks Jack assigned me, each day was more frustrating than the last. I knew the contract had been delayed and thought perhaps they were trying to keep me busy. I hated busy work.

Around May 2016, I transferred to a new department, working with Karl, the associate director, and Patricia, the director. Though I happily joined their team, I thought it was odd I wasn't assigned to them when I first came up to the third floor. Nevertheless, here I was, and the C.-Diff contract was coming any day.

In October 2016, CMS published new federal requirements that every long-term care facility (skilled nursing home) in the country had to have an Infection Prevention and Control Program (IPCP) in place by November 28, 2016 (Phase One), Antibiotic Stewardship Program by November 28,

2017 (Phase Two), and a professional (at least part-time) dedicated to infection control by November 28, 2019 (Phase Three).[12]

While I impatiently waited for the contract, I developed a data-driven analytic tracking tool to help our teams monitor each nursing home's progress for enrolling into NHSN. This laborious five-step process posed constant challenges. With over five hundred nursing homes to support in four states, I knew we needed a method to track what step each facility was on and for how long.

The contract was finally awarded around June of 2016. The scope of work involved recruiting at least 15 percent of the state's nursing homes, support them in enrolling into NHSN, having them report baseline C.-Diff data for one year, and then report another year of C.-Diff data with targeted quality improvement. The overall goal was to reduce a state's C.-Diff rates. It all looked good on paper, with the timelines, budget, and staffing appearing feasible.

However, CMS didn't account for the enormous challenges that the nursing homes would face when enrolling into NHSN. On the national calls that I'd attend with the other QIOs, the staff working with the nursing homes would complain about how hard it was to figure out or get help with the process. "They [nursing homes] won't even take the time to call me back," I would hear, or "They ignore my calls," or "This isn't that hard, why can't they just *do* it?" They were referring to the five-step process of enrollment. In actuality, there were more like twelve steps, as each of the five steps had its own sub-steps.

When my data tracking tool identified that 90 percent of our nursing homes were stuck in their enrollment process at the step where the CDC had to issue a unique SAMS grid card, assigned to each person, we were able to notify CMS, our client, that the entire project was headed for a global failure. Because we were keeping track of each step and were able to offer the graphical representation of our standstill to CMS, they extended the enrollment period from six weeks to six months. This was a big deal in the QIN-QIO world, as they work on rigid time frames.

During the entire project, I found myself running as fast and hard as I could to help the nursing homes. I was often flown out to our sister state to support their teams in the process of getting the facilities enrolled when they were falling behind. It wasn't a project for the faint of heart; nothing ever is within our healthcare setting. The QIO's Executive Director, Alex, used to call me Secretariat, as I had a drive to work at top speed with maximum effort to succeed in helping these facilities.

Nursing home staff are constantly being pulled in many directions, and often one of those directions is toward an emergency. This is often how I felt as a mother of five, so understanding and empathy for them came easily. When I called the nursing homes to assist them, I would hear in the background the hectic soundtrack of a nursing home worker's day: residents yelling, alarms going off, phones ringing, and so on. They were swamped, and we, the QIOs, were upset because they didn't have the time to stop everything, including caring for the residents, to enroll in a program that had technical issues and was notorious for breaking down or not working at the precise moment they needed it.

A colleague suggested I create short three-to-five-minute videos that the nursing homes could view to help with the complicated enrollment process. Knowing how busy they were and that the current CDC training was over an hour, this was a great recommendation. I set out to create training videos that were easy to follow, with step-by-step instructions for the process. Creating a short training video for a highly technical and complicated process proved an enormous challenge. It took me several takes to get in the flow and not appear too stiff. Filming proved to be the easy part; then came the voice-over editing and animation.

We created these videos right away and distributed them to our nursing homes and the thirteen other QIOs. They were an instant hit. The nursing homes loved the videos as they could pull them up anywhere, even on their phones and at home. They were so precise that they simplified the enrollment process for thousands of nursing homes. It took about one to two weeks to complete one step of the enrollment process, so I did my best to stay one step ahead of the national enrollment so I could offer the training. The CDC loved the training videos so much that they joined my process, providing feedback on the scripts prior to filming.

Given the success, we knew we needed additional videos for conducting C.-Diff surveillance, reporting C.-Diff to NHSN, and using the data for action. In all, we created thirteen videos.[13]

After six months, over 15 percent of nursing homes across the country had successfully enrolled, approximately 3,600 facilities. This was a dramatic increase from only 2 percent (around three hundred nursing homes) previously enrolled in NHSN.[14]

Chief Medical Officer, Dr. Michael Wasserman, recalls that he knew this would be the "hardest lift in the history of the QIOs." It was. His team consisted of five staff members who had worked intimately with the California nursing homes for many years.

"We all took the work very seriously and knew that getting the nursing homes to report C.-Diff data into NHSN could really promote change," Wasserman said.

From the inception of the project, in the QIO world, we believed this pilot study was only the beginning of a new federal requirement that would be the future for nursing homes reporting their HAI data into NHSN, as was necessary for acute care settings. In fact, this was one of our recruitment messages: "Best to get on this while you have the free support from the QIO and before it's mandatory." One nursing home administrator, fed up with all of the phone calls and "strategic harassment" to get them to meet "our" CMS deadlines, responded to my messages with "I don't care if it's eventually going to be required, it's not now, and there are other priorities."

Believe me, I understood. It did feel like we were harassing the nursing homes most of the time, as it would take dozens of reminder emails and phone calls to get them to complete enrollment and then enter their monthly data on time. We simply thought there was no way that CMS would *not* make this a requirement for nursing homes. They had to, otherwise why go to all this trouble?

In March of 2018, I was invited to attend the CDC's Epidemiology and Laboratory Capacity Health Care Association Infections/Antibiotic Resistance conference in Atlanta, Georgia. This annual meeting is one that an epidemiologist from every state's health department attends. The CDC asked me to share my experience working with nursing homes and the success of enrolling them into NHSN to report their C.-Diff data. I felt a bit like a fish out of water because there was only one other person from a QIO in attendance. I did not, however, let this intimidate me or slow my drive to communicate the message of getting 100 percent of our nation's nursing homes enrolled into NHSN. I saw this day as an opportunity to let these at the top levels know what my mission was.

After the first morning break, I marched up to the Director of the Division of Healthcare Quality Promotion (DHQP) and introduced myself. I described our accomplishments as a QIO and my passion for expanding the work into all nursing homes. She agreed this was an important initiative and thanked me for all the work we were doing. I gave her my business card, writing on the back so that she would remember me, "Passionate about NHSN!!"

I also introduced myself to the Associate Director of the CDC's HAI prevention program, Dr. Arjun Srinivasan, MD and quickly asked, "How do we get every nursing home enrolled into NHSN?"

"We need to hear the voice of the nursing homes," he said. "That reporting into NHSN is helping them with improved antibiotic stewardship, infection control, and infection prevention practices. If you can go back to your facilities and see if they'll submit a testimonial, then we can submit that to CMS. This will support the need to move this forward."

"Done!" I said confidently. I was willing to go the distance, so asking for a few testimonials seemed like a piece of cake.

Back home, I asked permission from my leadership if I could indeed reach out and request testimonials from the nursing homes. They responded that since we'd already asked so much of them (like enrollment into NHSN), they were concerned that we shouldn't ask them for more. While this was true, it didn't quite make sense. We had good working relationships with our nursing homes, and I knew they'd rather do this small favor. So, I asked anyway. I was more interested in pushing the work forward on a national level.

I asked twenty nursing homes for a testimonial and received ten back in response. All ten conveyed that the work we were doing was helpful, supportive, and made a difference. They conveyed the need for a data reporting program and the support that was provided by the QIO.

Those of us working on the nursing home initiative knew this was where we were headed, and we strongly advocated for the advancement of this work. We knew it would be an incredible waste not to transform all the work into a new federal requirement. Why do it at all and spend the resources building this tool if not to complete the project? Unfortunately, this is not what happened.

Shortly after the CDC/HAI conference, and after two years of reporting the C.-Diff data, the work ended. It didn't appear that the testimonials or advocates for NHSN reporting had any effect. On May 19, 2018, I was called into the boardroom one morning and told that the nursing home work appeared steady and that my expertise was now needed on the hospital Health Improvement Innovation Network (HIIN) collaborative to support hospitals reporting Opioid data. They basically wanted to use my "Secretariat" energy to get hospitals to report data not currently being captured with their electronic health records. Knowing my absolute passion was with the nursing homes, and that I had only begun to make an impact where it was needed most, I resigned from my position and started my own consulting firm.

This was the scariest step that I had ever taken, but I knew the nursing homes needed support and I was dedicated to standing strong and not giving up, no matter the cost.

I was head- and heart-strong, ready to support the country in getting all nursing homes enrolled into NHSN, not only to report C.-Diff but other infections such as UTIs and multidrug resistant organisms such as MRSA.

Unfortunately, the government was not on board with this vision. When the new five-year CMS quality improvement contracts came out in the summer of 2019, the entire QIO budget was cut by 80 percent, nearly decimating the QIOs. Massive layoffs would ensue with many of my former colleagues scrambling to find work. The nursing home infection control support was minuscule with the initiative to continue enrolling nursing homes into NHSN and reporting their infections completely gone. The three-year project that pioneered the way forward to finally understanding the true burden of infections in nursing homes was over. Little did policymakers know, a global disaster loomed, heading toward us in six short months. In a conversation I later had with Dr. Wasserman, he said, "Can you imagine if we had carried on and built on the NHSN network, where nursing homes might have been at the onset of the pandemic? Hundreds if not thousands of lives could have been saved had we marched on and carried this work forward."

CHAPTER 4

INFECTION DEFLECTION PRIOR TO THE PANDEMIC

"Plan ahead or find trouble on the doorstep."

—Confucius

It was the last day of the CDC's National Healthcare Safety Network (NHSN) training for the nursing homes, to which I'd been invited to discuss my experience working with nursing homes during the C.-Diff project. That morning I was presenting easy-to-implement solutions to capture and report C.-Diff data to NHSN. I was excited because my good friend Dr. Nimalie Stone, a board-certified infectious disease physician and the Medical Epidemiologist for the Long-term Care Division of Quality Promotion at the CDC, had asked the day before if we could meet for breakfast. It would be our last opportunity to get together before I had to leave town.

Nimalie shared my passion for helping nursing homes implement infection control programs. A strong advocate for the nursing home industry, Nimalie helped develop infection prevention and control programs and policies.[1]

It was a muggy day on the way to the restaurant, The General Muir, where we chose to talk shop. She shared with me the challenges of having nursing homes continue reporting their C.-Diff data into NHSN, especially since the national project was nearing its end. This wasn't a huge surprise to me, given the copious number of man-hours required to keep the project going. With a limited CMS budget, QIOs couldn't maintain a sufficient workforce for the project to support the nursing homes' continued reporting of infectious disease data. What struck me about Nimalie was her tenacity; much like my own, she was never willing to throw in the towel.

Dr. Stone worked in the industry her entire career, including completing her internal medicine residency at Johns Hopkins University and providing infection prevention and control clinical counsel at Emory's geriatric hospital and nursing home at West Woods Center. She's no stranger to the challenges within long-term care and the growing rate at which infectious diseases are plaguing this industry. Dr. Stone's work has focused on decreasing the inappropriate prescribing of antibiotics in nursing homes, which can then consequently reduce infections like C.-Diff and multi-drug resistant organisms, such as Carbapenem-resistant Enterobacteriaceae (CRE), bacteria that are commonly spread in healthcare settings and are resistant to a group of antibiotics known as carbapenems. The CDC has categorized CREs as urgent threats to public health.[2] Dr. Stone has contributed significantly to the national action plan for combating antibiotic resistance, specifically in nursing homes. As the long-term care team lead, she was overseeing the completion of the guidance on how to implement certain infection control protocols for new and emerging pathogens such as *Candida auris*, an emerging fungus that's becoming a global threat due to its resistance to antifungal medications; it's difficult to detect and is spreading rapidly in healthcare settings. It causes serious infections of the bloodstream and even death. Residents in nursing homes are at the highest risk for disease from this yeast, spread through the healthcare environment on surfaces, equipment, and from person to person.

In traditional acute settings, such as the hospital, patients are isolated to their hospital room anytime they're colonized with an infection, meaning the condition remains inactive in their body. It's a safety protocol to isolate patients in the event of an active, transmittable infection. This is not an appropriate safety protocol in a nursing home because we have residents who will live their remaining days there, and they would literally stay locked in their rooms forever. Nimalie wanted my opinion on the modified isolation protocol.

"Yes, of course," I said. "We simply can't keep them locked in their rooms forever." She wondered how the nursing home industry would respond to such a protocol.

"I believe they'd be relieved and grateful for the consideration of the unique environment," I told her. As always, I felt honored that Nimalie trusted what I had to say and looked to me for a "boots on the ground" perspective. Our conversation gave her more confidence that they were on the right track.

Nimalie was thrilled to hear I was doing so well with my new consulting firm and grateful I could run uninhibited to helping the nursing homes. I talked to her about my plan to enroll nursing homes into NHSN and start having them report not only C.-Diff data into NHSN but also their UTI data and process measures, such as hand hygiene, gown, and glove usage. We agreed that if we didn't measure the infections in this healthcare space, we would have little to no effect on making lasting change. It felt good to talk with a fellow warrior, an ally in combating the serious challenges nursing homes face.

My heart was full that morning after having such a dynamic conversation with Nimalie. I got up to the stage more passionate than ever to deliver some hope and sound advice to these nursing homes to help them with their infection control surveillance process and further their infection control program.

I'd met Dr. Patricia Stone, Ph.D. (no relation to Dr. Nimalie Stone), a nurse scientist and adult nurse practitioner, a few years back at an infection control national conference. I was impressed by her research on nursing homes and the role of the infection preventionist. Back then, she'd talked about the barriers to having a strong infection control program, including the lack of data reporting, staff turnover, education, and wages.

Dr. Stone lives in California and has commuted to New York over the years to conduct research out of Columbia University. She is an early pioneer of infection control research in healthcare settings, such as hospitals. In fact, the term "patient safety" was coined when she began her work in 2000. Relatively speaking, twenty years isn't that long ago; however, it was around that time that the healthcare industry still believed that getting an infection as a result of a hospital stay was normal practice and simply the risk posed when obtaining healthcare services. Dr. Stone spent about eight years working on the hospital side of infection control research and noticed that while there were many people in the space, nobody was conducting infection control research in nursing homes. Therefore, she started writing grants and began gathering research to evolve the IPC landscape in nursing homes.

Her team's nursing home research included estimating the total number of infections occurring in nursing homes. Prior estimates at the time were from decades-old data. Utilizing national data sources, such as the

Minimum Data Set (MDS) for clinical assessments (physical condition, psychological status, psychosocial functioning, and end-of-life care decisions) and CASPER data for the facility information for its size and other data sources, they were able to determine that around one to three million infections were occurring annually in nursing homes.[3] In addition, her team looked at the current infection prevention and control processes, such as hand hygiene and the appropriate use of personal protective equipment (PPE). They looked at IPC staffing and how it related to infection control processes and patient outcomes. Finally, qualitative interviews with the nursing home staff were conducted to augment the research. Her team knew that infections in this setting were a problem and that infection control practices were dismal.

I used a lot of Dr. Stone's research to support my doctoral research as there wasn't really much else out there. Her research motivated me to continue working in uncharted territory. Little did we both know how instrumental our work would be with a new and emerging virus on the horizon.

When I spoke with her recently, Dr. Stone said she learned of the "new virus" from China at the end of January 2020. She had a Chinese-American colleague from New York who was extremely worried. Her colleague told her to cancel her flight to New York and stay at home. At that point, Dr. Stone decided to stop her regular California-to-New-York commute. She recalls walking her dog with a good friend who asked her if "this coronavirus" would become a problem. This question made her think, *Is this a pandemic?* The World Health Organization hadn't yet declared it as such, but she thought it still checked the boxes defining a pandemic: it was an infectious disease in multiple countries, with no known cure.

She recalled having no idea it was going to be so big or devasting, impacting all of 2020 and continuing on into 2021.

But when in February 2020 she heard of thirty-eight residents dying of COVID in a nursing home in Kirkland, Washington, she knew we were in a serious situation with a virus that traveled like wildfire.

"It made my head spin," she later told me. "I was just stunned. Just stunned that it was that bad. I never thought it would be that bad."

Given her team's extensive research within nursing homes, she wasn't too surprised that nursing homes were not prepared for the virus. In 2014, there were less than 3 percent of nursing homes with a certified infection preventionist. In 2016, new infection control CMS federal regulations were only the beginning of change for the nursing home landscape. In 2018, the number of certified infections preventionists went up to 7 percent.[4] Dr. Stone's research demonstrated that if a facility had a trained IP along with certification, this truly made a difference for various infection control practices and processes like antibiotic stewardship, better outbreak policies, and UTI prevention.

"It all made a difference," Dr. Stone told me. "Thank God the regulations were in place. Things would have been a lot worse with this pandemic if we were back in 2014."

She suggested I talk with Dr. Lona Mody, M.D., M.Sc., another leading research pioneer in nursing home research. Dr. Mody is the University of Michigan's Amanda Sanford Hickey Professor of Internal Medicine, the Director of the Pepper Center Pilot and Exploratory Studies Core, the Associate Division Chief of the university's Geriatric and Palliative Care Medicine, and an Associate Director of Clinical Translational Research for the Geriatrics Center. Her research career began as a medical director for a nursing home in 2000, when she began applying for grants. Since 2002, she conducted her research in the nursing home setting, and she performed clinical work in both hospital geriatrics and internal medicine.

In 2007, Mody and her colleagues published a paper in the American

Geriatric Society that surveyed nursing home administrators in Nebraska and Michigan for pandemic preparedness.[5] Of those surveyed, only 25 percent had a pandemic plan. Given this information, Mody wrote a National Institute of Health (NIH) grant, which was not funded.

"It was just ahead of its time, I think," she said when we spoke. "But we wrote a road map on how to prepare for pandemics in nursing homes, making some assumptions. And several of those things came true this time, which is really a sad sort of thing, just because we thought about it and wrote about it and predicted some of this already."

As Dr. Mody described her extensive work, I was filled with gratitude for making nursing home care a priority. I asked her, given her expertise, what her first reaction was to the virus early on.

"I thought, *Oh my goodness, I hope this doesn't impact us*," she said.

She knew early on that, from a nursing home perspective, people weren't taking it as seriously as they should have. She had prayed, she said, that "nursing homes would be spared once again" as they'd been with the SARS 1 and SARS 2 epidemics.

Dr. Mody was inspired to paint, pouring her anxiety onto canvas that would eventually be published along with other pandemic paintings in a coffee table book called *Nature Medicine*.[6]

Not long after, I spoke with another important researcher, Dr. Tamara Konetzka, Ph.D., Professor of Health Economics and Health Services Research at the University of Chicago. When Dr. Konetzka first learned of the "new virus" from China and saw the outbreak in the Kirkland nursing home, she knew this would become a huge issue.

"My first thought—and we weren't alone in this thinking, as a lot of other researchers pursued this—was how do we figure out which nursing homes would be most at risk," she said. "We [researchers] needed a way to predict which nursing homes were going be in trouble. Obviously, we hoped to be able to direct assistance toward those nursing homes and figure out what to do to avoid the carnage that we began to see early on."

Dr. Konetzka testified before the United States Senate Special Committee on Aging in May of 2020, with preliminary data from this research. With twenty-five years of long-term and post-acute care research, she has served as the principal investigator for numerous federal grants and published many journal articles that examine nursing home quality and how public policy may drive improvement. Furthermore, Dr. Konetzka serves on the technical expert panel that advises CMS on the Nursing Home Compare website and five-star rating system. She testified before Congress about the disproportionate COVID-19 cases and deaths in nursing homes, which weren't surprising, given the communal living atmosphere and residents with multiple comorbidities that are often bed-bound and require hands-on daily care. Current systems of reporting, she emphasized, don't prioritize safety issues, including infection control.

Dr. Konetzka identified understaffing as a significant issue.

"Understaffing in nursing homes was a problem long before the pandemic," she reported. "Nurses' aides, who provide the majority of direct care to nursing home residents, are generally paid minimum wage and often have no paid sick leave or health insurance. Registered nurses, who provided essential oversight and diagnostic functions as well as skilled care, would often rather work in hospitals that usually offer higher wages and better working conditions. Even prior to the current emergency, nursing homes rarely possessed the staff capacity to address much milder challenges than those posed by the COVID-19 pandemic."[7]

Before the pandemic, inadequate infection control practices, such as inadequate handwashing and treatment of linens, were the most commonly cited deficiencies by nursing home inspectors. In fact, 82 percent of nursing homes were cited with having one or more infection control deficiencies between 2013 and 2017.[8] Therefore, it was clear early on that nursing homes would require technical assistance to ensure best infection control practices were implemented.

It's clear that infection control practices in nursing homes were a problem long before COVID-19, and yet nursing homes received little support in resolving this problem. The consequences of not having a solid—or any, in some cases—IPC program in place became painfully apparent when COVID-19 began to make its way into US nursing homes.

CHAPTER 5

FIGHTING A WAR WITHOUT ARMOR

"If you don't have PPE, it's game over."

—Michael Wasserman, M.D.

COVID-19 has changed our world forever. None of us could ever have anticipated the impact this deadly virus was going to have on our lives. And it was evident that nursing homes didn't have a grasp on good infection control practices or adequate pandemic preparedness before COVID-19. The result carried devastating consequences, and an enormously disproportionate number of people lost their lives. Four percent of the US population lives in nursing homes, yet 31 percent of all US COVID deaths are linked to nursing homes.[1]

Let's pause and take that in. These are human lives, not statistics on a page. Our vulnerable family and friends, and the dedicated staff that cared for them were involuntarily exposed to and died from an invisible enemy.

As I've mentioned, in early January 2020, I started hearing about the emerging virus coming out of Wuhan, China. But it was the middle of the influenza season, and I was focused on advocating for nursing homes to achieve high influenza vaccination compliance and busy raising awareness around the millions of other infections occurring in nursing homes. But suddenly, there was this "novel" virus across the world that was grabbing people's attention.

The CDC was reporting the COVID-19 virus as "airborne," which means germs or pathogens are small enough to remain suspended in the air for up to three hours and transmit over distances greater than six feet. For example, tuberculosis, a bacterium that can attack the lungs, can remain suspended in the air after someone has coughed for up to six hours. This is different from droplet transmission, which occurs when a person sneezes, coughs, or exhales large respiratory "droplets" of a virus or bacteria that can only travel a short distance (less than six feet). Contact transmission occurs when a person with an infectious bacteria or virus touches or exchanges bodily fluids with someone who can transmit a disease, such as pink eye. Indirect contact transmission can also occur if an individual touches an object with an infectious agent on its surface, such as C.-Diff spores, which can remain on a surface for up to five months. In a healthcare setting, the precautions and personal protection equipment (PPE) used depends on the mode of transmission for a specific virus or infection.

When the CDC first reported COVID-19, the healthcare community was told that all patients should be placed on airborne precautions, meaning that any person entering the patient's room should wear a gown, fit-tested N95 respirator, eye protection, and gloves. In addition, the patient would be in a special room called a negative air pressure room that pulled air out through the ventilation system. In addition, a respiratory protection program was required by the Occupational Safety and Health Act

(OSHA) that included fit-testing any individuals wearing an N95 respirator. Fit testing is a method designed to ensure the tight-fitting respirator fits the user appropriately to provide the adequate level of protection from pathogens. If it doesn't fit, it doesn't work.

Most, perhaps all US nursing homes, have safety measures in place for controlling infections by droplet or contact transmission. Airborne vectors are difficult to control unless the facility has installed a working "negative air ventilation system," or expects staff to use specific PPE such as a fit-tested N95 respirator.

If this level of care was being required for patients with COVID-19, then nursing home staff and management assumed COVID-infected patients would have to go to the hospital, given nursing homes do not care for patients that require this level of care. They do not have negative air pressure rooms, do not have a respiratory protection program in place, nor have the training or equipment to fit-test healthcare workers to wear the N95 respirator.

In early March 2020, my home state of Arizona downgraded the required isolation precautions for COVID-19 from airborne to droplet and contact. This meant that a nursing home *could* care for a resident that had or was recovering from COVID-19. The state did maintain that if any resident required aerosolized procedures, such as a respiratory breathing treatment which can suspend droplets in the air for longer periods, then an N95 respirator and eye protection like goggles or face shields were recommended for all healthcare workers that came into contact with infected patients, to prevent their mucous membranes (eyes, nose, and mouth) from becoming infected (because this is a mode of transmission of this virus). I knew that many residents who were on breathing treatments with a small volume nebulizer (SVN), CPAP-, and BiPAP-produced aerosols could potentially be infectious. In response to this, many residents were immediately switched to a single-dose inhaler to eliminate the risk of producing infectious aerosols.

Being proactive, I texted Samantha, a fellow infection preventionist colleague of mine who worked in a hospital, and asked if I could send over a few infection preventionists to get N95 fit-tested and trained to fit-test their staff. My request was denied; her hospital wasn't even able to keep up with their own staffing needs.

Having previously worked in nursing homes during the 2003 severe acute respiratory syndrome (SARS) outbreak, Samantha described her experience with SARS caused by a coronavirus. SARS was first reported in February 2003 in Asia, she reminded me, and rapidly spread to twenty-four additional countries, resulting in over 8,000 individuals being infected and 774 dying.[2] SARS was primarily transmitted through close person-to-person contact when someone sneezed or coughed, as well as through contact when someone touched an infected surface. Samantha warned me that, given all this, COVID-19 was certain to spread like wildfire through nursing homes.

Then it happened.

On February 29, 2020, news broke about that nursing home in Kirkland, Washington. Life Care Center of America, situated in a Seattle suburb, was the first official COVID-19 outbreak. Fifteen days before the outbreak, the nursing staff noticed a cluster of residents with the same respiratory symptoms spreading through the facility. Sick residents were sent to nearby EvergreenHealth hospital. They thought they had an outbreak of pneumonia and, at this point, had no COVID-19 tests to confirm the virus. Testing was limited to the CDC's lab in Atlanta and was reserved for people that had traveled to China. None of the patients in EvergreenHealth qualified. Life Care Center of America would prove to be ground zero for the US.[3]

On March 4, 2020, I got a call from Roger, the regional manager for four Arizona nursing homes in the area whose facilities I'd just begun to work. Roger described how one of the nursing homes had two residents with highly contagious C.-Diff. It is worth repeating that C.-Diff spores are hardy and can live for up to five months on surfaces; therefore, when a resident has C.-Diff, they're placed on contact precautions, which means anyone entering the resident's room must wear a clean gown and new gloves. Every single person, every single time. Furthermore, prior to leaving the resident's room, all the PPE is removed and disposed of.

The gown is critical to preventing the cross-contamination or spreading of this bacterium. Roger's staff had no gowns.

In over twenty-five years working in healthcare, I'd never heard of a nursing home that didn't have access to the PPE they needed to perform their work safely. Before COVID, my uphill battle was educating the staff about when and how to appropriately use PPE, as there's a correct process for putting it on (donning) and taking it off (doffing). Now a new fight-within-a-fight began, one where the soldiers were not only fighting the war but doing so without weapons and armor.

Roger texted me saying that they were going to purchase long-sleeve, washable lab coats because they were unable to get any supplies.

"Lab coats?" I asked. "No! I don't want you wearing lab coats. We need to find you disposable gowns!"

Roger thought it ironic that we'd only started talking a few days ago, and the better part of his days were already taken up with infection control.

"This is making me rethink how I want to roll out your service," he said.

Not long after this, I reached out to the county health department and left a message letting them know of this emerging situation—that the nursing home was in desperate need of PPE. This was the earliest step in the hierarchy of command. First, you reach out to your county, then the state health department. Because I couldn't get anyone on the phone, I sent an email to the state health department.

> Hi All!
>
> Do you have any recommendations for healthcare facilities that are running critically low on PPE? I have a client that has residents on isolation and is running low, and their distributor is *sold out.*
>
> Thanks for your help.

Having worked with the department for many years, I had relationships with the epidemiology department and was sure they'd respond fast.

They did. The department's senior epidemiologist responded by emailing me an Excel spreadsheet that had circulated around the state to identify the whereabouts of PPE.

Great, I thought. I now had a list of healthcare settings with extra supplies. I began making phone calls from the database, and to my dismay, *nobody* had PPE to offer. In fact, every facility that put its name on the spreadsheet had a shortage of PPE, not an overstock. I reached out to hospitals in local areas to see if their distributors had supplies. There were none available. Everyone was in preservation mode and didn't want to let go of anything.

Roger wasn't having any luck either. "I'm way out of my depth here," he texted me. "It's interesting that a major manufacturer of PPE is China. I fear this is only the beginning of what might be a very long drought."

While Roger contacted McKesson and Medline, the largest distributors of nursing home supplies, I reached out to the vendors I knew. We both received the same response: There was no PPE available. In the interim,

Roger's staff began duct-taping large garbage bags together to create makeshift gowns, offering at least some protection.

My head was spinning. I couldn't believe that duct-taping trash bags had become our reality. I called the county health department several more times, to no avail. The next morning, and desperate for help, I emailed Dr. Nimalie Stone and the long-term care team, hoping for some assistance, and got an "out of office" response. Panic set in. I tried the state health department again, this time with a bolded and highlighted email.

> Hi All,
>
> We have reached out to the contacts on the list with no luck. Everyone that has PPE is "holding" on to it because they are afraid of not having what they need. Any other suggestions? I reached out to the County yesterday but only had the option to leave a phone message. I have not heard back from them. I have reached out to the CDC's Long-term Care team as well. Currently, the facility is using one lab coat per resident for PPE. They even duct-taped garbage bags together. There has to be more that we can do to help!!

Within five minutes of sending the email, I got a call from the Executive Director of the Arizona Hospital and Healthcare Association (AzHHA), and then the Bureau Chief from the state health department, saying that PPE supplies from McKesson were on backorder until they could be "released."

Then, just as quickly, came a call from Diane Eckles with the State Licensing Division. Diane is the Arizona Bureau Chief for the CMS nursing home regulatory division. I'd never received a personal phone call from Diane, and my heart was racing when I answered; I figured this was in reference to the rumblings I was making regarding my client's facility and the lack of PPE.

"What is this I hear about a nursing home with C.-Diff residents and no gowns? This is an automatic IJ," she said. An IJ or "immediate jeopardy" is the most severe citation a nursing home can get from the state regulatory division. I'm sure my face went red, and my heart rate and blood pressure increased. I explained how I'd spent over twenty-four hours doing everything I knew to get this facility the appropriate PPE, including reaching out to local, state, and federal public health officials, and licensing called me to warn me of a punishment and tell me they could be in trouble.

Diane apologized, saying she wasn't aware of what had occurred in the past twenty-four hours and thought a "complaint" had come in.

"No!" I explained. "The facility and I had been sending emails and making phone calls in hopes of finding supplies." Diane ended our conversation by promising that help was on its way. But now I was worried that state licensing was involved. Had I gone too far by emailing the CDC? I certainly didn't want to get the nursing home in trouble.

I called Roger and described the morning events and the call from Diane, which had ended well. I said I didn't think his staff was at any risk of getting in trouble. He thanked me for fighting hard for the facility and told me not to worry.

Two hours later, the nursing home received two cases of XXL gowns.

"Oh, praise God!" I said.

I then received an email from the county:

> Update: County Public Health Emergency Preparedness received a call on 3/5/20 at 10:07 a.m. with the request for assistance from XYZ Nursing Center. County health made contact with the DON at XYZ Nursing Center to determine immediate needs...we were able to obtain

> and provide them with 300 earloop masks 108 XXL surgical gowns (6 boxes), and 30 L surgical gowns (1 box) cache supply from H1N1 stored at the hospital warehouse....Delivery of the items was made at 12:00 p.m. today. Discussion followed to contact the local health department or healthcare coalition when resources are needed in the future for a *faster response.*

I was beyond grateful that the supplies were being delivered but frustrated by the statement to contact the local health department or coalition for a *faster response*. That's exactly what we had done!

Still, I could breathe a bit easier now knowing PPE would protect the healthcare workers while caring for residents with a highly infectious disease. Had I known what was to come in the days, weeks, months, and years ahead, I'd have conserved my energy. This was only the beginning of a fight to obtain the necessary resources and support for nursing homes during what would become a global crisis.

From that day forward, I received calls nearly every day from nursing homes in a PPE crisis. Sarah, an infection preventionist, had me on speed dial; we talked nearly every day. A nurse for ten years (nine of them in long-term care), she worked in a nursing home in a rural community in Northern Arizona. Prior to taking on the infection preventionist role in 2018, she had other positions, including assistant director of nurses (ADON), MDS coordinator, floor nurse, and interim director of nurses (DON). She'd always loved geriatric nursing because she believed the elderly were a forgotten generation of people, often dismissed and not given dignity at the end of their lives. As someone close to her own grandparents, she made caring for this generation her priority.

Before COVID-19, Sarah's biggest concerns in infection control had been getting the staff to conduct hand hygiene and managing healthcare workers who showed up to work sick. She and I had worked together for over a year, and Sarah had made great strides in her infection prevention and control (IPC) program. She understood the importance of how the non-clinical staff, such as housekeepers, needed a lot of extra IPC training.

When she first heard of the new virus, Sarah shared the hope that many of us did: it wouldn't come to the US. At the same time I began my quest for obtaining PPE, she got the call from her administrator saying they needed to lock down the facility per a new CMS requirement.

"It makes me want to cry, thinking about it," she told me. "We had to post signs on the facility entrance, stating that no visitors were allowed. It was horrible."

It was a Sunday in mid-March when Sarah's nursing home got their first sick patient.

"That's when the hell started," she told me. "We worked constantly from then on."

Prior to going to work that day, she'd had a conversation with her husband. She told him that she didn't know what they were facing, or if she would have to "live" at the nursing home. "I remember him looking at me saying, 'We are not going to live our lives like that, we are going to be together, and we will just take our chances.' I remember crying at home because I was terrified. I remember getting to work after a twenty-minute drive and basically leaving my emotions in my car and saying, 'You have to suck it up.' I had to walk into our facility and act like nothing was wrong, and that we would be fine, we were brave and had the PPE we needed to do it right."

Sarah also remembers the early support—or lack of support—from the county health department. She called the epidemiologist over the weekend and asked what she was supposed to do with a COVID-19 swab laboratory test from her patient. The lab was closed, and the local hospital would not accept it.

His response was grim: "Oh, you have to wait a couple of days until the lab is open."

Sarah responded, "So, what do I do in the meantime?"

"Just isolate him."

It was then apparent to Sarah that the county epidemiologist didn't know what to do, and the call ended with him saying, "I really don't know what else to tell you."

During this time, Sarah and her team worked for more than seventy days straight. I remember working with her during those early days; the constant communication via phone and text messaging—night and day, weekday and weekend. With little to no support from public health, Sarah, like many other nursing home infection preventionists, had to get creative with her COVID-19 action plan.

"Okay, don't laugh, but here's what we did," Sarah told me one morning over the phone. "We set up our COVID unit in our dining room."

"Laugh?" I replied. "Hell, that's just brilliant."

"It was for only one resident," she went on, "and we didn't want to move everyone else around. She was the first resident that tested positive, and yet she was asymptomatic. I'm still not sure if she ever had it. This was when testing was so weird. The county was making us test everyone because of potential exposure, and she was positive. She had no respiratory symptoms."

"She was our first *dining room* patient," Sarah explained. "God, there were these horrible tarps we'd set up. Looking back, it looked like death. So dark, but it was a perfect ward. It reminded me of what they may have had during war times; stack as many patients as you can. We could take in eight patients; we had eight bays. But we had no bathroom in our makeshift COVID unit. Everything was sealed with a dedicated staff and no toilet. We used a temporary, portable commode and a bucket with kitty litter. It was horrible for the nurses."

"Wait," I said to Sarah. "Kitty litter?"

"To help solidify the waste," Sarah explained. "Thank God the resident was continent and could manage the commode herself, because we had only one staff member in there. The nurses told me the worst part wasn't the lack of PPE or the isolation from everyone else. It was dumping that bucket of urine and poop. It was bad, just bad!"

Luckily, Sarah's facility didn't completely run out of PPE. The owners spent whatever was necessary to get the staff what they needed. Sarah recalls seeing a bill for $5,000 for one day, $7,000 the next. They bought air purifiers and participated in an initiative that I, along with SPH Medical, would eventually get off the ground.

Dr. Patricia Stone recalls that resources such as PPE were going to the hospitals or nursing homes affiliated with a hospital at that time. If you were a small mom-and-pop nursing home and trying to buy your own PPE, you were on your own. The government efforts were an incompetent attempt at providing most nursing homes with the critical supplies they so desperately needed.

Unlike the nursing home where Sarah worked, most were unable to secure supplies. I heard about this from nursing home employees daily. As the 2019 Chapter President of the Association for Professionals in Infection Control and Epidemiology (AZ APIC), I had a database of over one hundred vendors I hoped would help replenish PPE supplies. I reached out to them frequently, and always with no success. The limited supplies were first offered to hospitals. Bidding wars began between state governors trying to secure PPE supplies.

More commonly, vendors told me it would take a large order of over fifty thousand pieces to ensure I could get the supplies—an impossible ask for the smaller organizations I tried to support. A typical PPE order consisted of tens of thousands of N95 respirators and gowns at prices a smaller facility couldn't afford.

For example, a typical PPE order had to have the following requirements:

- N95 Masks: *fifty thousand units.* Price: $4.75 (+/–) = $237,500.00
- KN95 Masks: *twenty-five thousand units.* Price: $3.25 (+/–) = $81,250.00
- LI ISO Gowns: *fifty thousand units min.* Price: $4.20 (+/–) = $210,000.00
- Total amount of this order: $528,750.00

It all seemed hopeless. And things were just getting started.

The sympathetic public expressed outrage about PPE supplies not being available to hospitals. Yet somehow the media didn't focus on the lack of critical equipment in nursing homes, but rather offered a skewed message about how many people were dying in these "death traps."

By the end of April, the United States was on full alert; many places were locked down, and travel was limited. And for me, the pandemic turned personal because my daughter Katie was about to give birth to my first grandchild in Knoxville, Tennessee.

At first, we didn't think I could come for the birth, given the lockdown in most states and the unknowns we all faced. Finally, a colleague said to me, "Buffy, you know what to do to protect yourself. You have to go." I arranged to arrive two weeks before Katie's due date so that I could quarantine. I let Sarah know, and she was kind enough to mail me an N95 duckbill respirator in a small paper bag, with a note that read, "Stay healthy! Enjoy your new grandbaby!"—such a kind gesture.

There were only eight people on my flight to Knoxville, none of whom wore any facial covering, including the flight attendants.

I was shocked. "Wait!" I wanted to shout. "We're in the middle of a global pandemic, and you're not wearing a face mask?"

To make matters worse, while I was waiting to board my flight, I overheard an unmasked traveling nurse telling a ticket agent he wasn't worried about COVID. I was appalled. *People are dying in record numbers, I thought to myself, and you're not worried?*

I stayed in a cozy rental about eight minutes from Katie and close to downtown amenities. Katie, now thirty-eight weeks pregnant, came over the first night to visit. What a beautiful site it was to see her standing in front of me, an opportunity I nearly missed. We both wore face masks, were socially distanced, and visited outdoors. This was not how I imagined life as a new grandma, but anything was better than nothing.

During my fourteen-day quarantine, I worked in the apartment and took daily walks, careful to avoid contact with others. I had my groceries delivered and stayed hunkered down.

One afternoon, I was having a phone conversation with my dad, explaining the crisis of limited PPE supplies in nursing homes, and how the vendors refused to take smaller orders. He suggested I reach out to a national news station such as CNN or FOX News and bring this to their attention.

"First, though, give the vendors one more chance," he suggested. "Reach out to them again and tell them you'll take it public if they won't budge."

Being an attorney, my dad is quite bold. That's probably where my interest in justice, fairness, and advocacy come from. Maybe he was right. Maybe taking this information to the media would help, perhaps give them a different perspective regarding the challenges in the nursing homes.

As soon as we hung up, I emailed several vendors I'd previously spoken to who had mentioned the possibility of getting PPE in bulk.

Good afternoon Valued Vendors,

I am reaching out to ask for your help! Our nursing homes are in dire need of personal protective equipment and infection control products such as hand sanitizer. They continue to go through their local vendors and public health but are still coming up severely short, resorting to items like raincoats and garbage bags for gowns. *Can you help?*

Our most vulnerable population deserves this as well as our staff working on the front line. Currently, half of all COVID-19 deaths are coming from nursing homes, yet they simply *do not* have what they need.

If you can *donate* any supplies, we will be sure they get to facilities that continue to tell us they are running out.

We are in *need* of the following:

- Hand sanitizer
- Gowns (disposable or launderable)
- Masks (Surgical, N95 for healthcare workers; cloth masks for residents)

Out of the dozens of vendors I sent this to, only one responded, SPH Medical. They wrote that they could order in bulk only—an answer I'd had before.

Tony Coleman (owner) and Stephen Caldwell (senior vice president of sales) were with SPH Medical, a safety-focused company that promotes the protection of healthcare workers. Tony and I first connected late in 2019. He had scheduled a call with me because my website encouraged visitors to "Schedule a twenty-minute consultation." During that conversation, I remembered Tony's great passion for supporting healthcare workers with the supplies they needed. We briefly discussed working together in the future.

Wanting to clarify their "bulk only" response, I sent this follow-up email:

> Hi Tony and Stephen,
>
> Can you explain to me why you are only offering PPE in bulk? Is there no way to get them to nursing homes in need?? We have people dying every day and healthcare workers getting sick because they do not have the appropriate PPE. Can you do anything to help us?

This call to action got Tony and Stephen's attention, and a phone call was scheduled.

I learned that right at the start of the pandemic, SPH Medical went into sourcing mode to help their immediate customers—hospitals and nursing homes (but mostly hospitals). They knew that they had to extend their domestic reach out to an international one and began contracting with manufacturers overseas to get PPE as quickly as possible.

The reality was that the market was going crazy, and everybody thought this was going to be an opportunity to make money, regardless of whether they were involved in the medical industry. Tony realized that it would be necessary to mobilize and adapt as quickly as possible, which meant completely rethinking how to approach the challenge in front of them and try to become part of a solution for a much bigger problem. They couldn't continue to let supplies go to the highest bidder.

Tony told me: "It essentially became an auction for a very limited amount of supply—it's David versus Goliath. And Chinese and other Asian or foreign factories produce this stuff. The vast majority is not made in the United States, which creates a scenario where, if you have money, say hundred-dollar bills in the back of a semi-truck, and you roll up to the factory, you're going to get the product before anyone else. That's how these manufacturing facilities work overseas." He went on to say, "Those are all things we had to contend with at the time, and it was constant adaptation, hour-by-hour, day-by-day, trying to secure these supplies."

Tony went completely out of the box and looked at the situation from a principal versus a financial standpoint. He knew that everything was on the table, and explained, "It was completely rethinking and establishing new partnerships, new relationships with factories and suppliers, and dealing with all of these backlogs and the uncertainty of international supply chains."

Tony educated me on the reality of getting supplies, and I educated him on the reality of the dire situation in nursing homes.

No one, and I mean no one, was delivering PPE in small quantities, and SPH wanted to solve that problem. We put our heads together and developed a process to get nursing homes the supplies they needed by creating a large order, pulling from many small nursing homes at once. This gave SPH enough buying power to compete with the massive health systems and government agencies. There were limited resources, yet everyone deserved to get the supplies that they needed.

Eventually, FEMA provided PPE for nursing homes, but it was incredibly shoddy and ineffective. The blue paper "capes" were useless, as were the dark blue tarps with a hole for a staff member's head to poke through—no armholes, nothing to tie it back. It was oversized, bulky, and impossible to use in a manner that would protect the healthcare staff.

"Even when the federal government stepped in to provide PPE, it was dismal and poor quality," recalls Dr. Patricia Stone. Echoing that, Dr. Konetzka said, "Facilities had maybe one week's worth of PPE, and others were making deals with Southwest Airlines. These efforts for procurement were ridiculous, and it put nursing homes' well-being on the line."

Ten Arizona nursing homes took advantage of our plan for combining small orders to create a larger one. This alleviated their PPE shortages.

On the heels of the PPE crisis, in June, CMS issued a memorandum to all nursing homes requiring them to report all COVID-19 infections, deaths, and PPE supply shortages into the CDC's National Healthcare Safety Network.[4] As you will recall, getting the nursing homes to report data into NHSN was what I, along with my colleagues, had been trying to achieve prior to the pandemic. Now, in the middle of this crisis, they *had* too. Poor timing for the nursing homes, but a necessary step in tracking COVID-19 and the PPE shortages.

The memorandum went on to describe the initiative to tie Coronavirus Aid, Relief, and Economic Security (CARES) Act grant monies to how well the facility was performing.[5] Basically, a quality improvement project. This would be determined by in-person surveys from the state licensing and regulatory division. Penalties for infection control non-compliance were being enhanced to "provide greater accountability and consequence for failure to meet these basic requirements."

I have to pause here for reflection, and so do you.

Do you, does anyone, think creating a performance-based program tied to monetary funding in the middle of a global pandemic is appropriate?

No.

Next, I have to address the quote: "...failure to meet basic requirements."

There is and was *nothing* basic about the COVID-19 pandemic. This was not a normal scenario under any circumstances; therefore, why in God's name did the federal regulatory office think for one minute that anything "normal" or, as they put it, "basic" was even an option?

Finally, Quality Improvement Organizations (QIO) were deployed to provide an array of assistance to low-performing nursing homes by offering weekly national infection control training, and the CDC would provide guidance and technical assistance to improve infection control practices to nursing homes and state health departments. Remote technical support was good but wouldn't go far enough to help the nursing homes. And the government made $11 billion in new funding available to states, territories, and localities to focus on COVID-19 testing in nursing homes and other vulnerable communities.[6] But testing kits wouldn't reach nursing homes until August 2020.

Things were just starting to heat up.

CHAPTER 6

DOCTORS WITHOUT BORDERS: DETROIT, MI

"They [nursing homes] don't have a right to object [to admitting covid-19 residents]. That is the rule and the regulations, and they have to comply with that."
—Former Governor Andrew Cuomo, New York, April 25, 2020

Early on in the pandemic, fears materialized as the transmission-based precautions were downgraded to droplet/contact from airborne. Nursing homes were, in some states, forced to take COVID-19 patients. And they were forced to take those patients whether or not they had PPE supplies, whether or not the staff was prepared, whether or not they even had the staff to care for the residents.

* * *

My daughter Katie gave birth to a beautiful, healthy baby boy, Adrian, on May 3, 2020. I was blessed to be able to stay at her home for two weeks and help with the baby while she and her husband adjusted. I will always cherish those days. I left Knoxville on May 18 to return to Phoenix.

Up until this point, I had been doing my work behind the scenes of the pandemic. Now it was time to get out from behind the computer, roll up my sleeves, and go where my skills were most needed: on-site at nursing homes.

Within days of returning home, I received an email from a colleague telling me that Doctors Without Borders (DWB) was looking to create a small team to travel and support nursing homes in the US and were looking for an IPC manager to join the team for a month, possibly longer.

This was exactly the opportunity I was ready for. It had been a childhood dream of mine to work with Doctors Without Borders, and within days I was interviewing with the New York office recruiter, Rogier, over Skype. Doctors Without Borders is the English name for Médecins Sans Frontières or MSF for short.

Based in France, MSF provides humanitarian services in under-served, poverty-stricken regions such as Liberia, Haiti, South Sudan, and the Congo but had never been in the US during its more-than-fifty years of existence.[1]

However, with international travel and borders closed, they thought it was an excellent time to have a US-based mission. They deployed teams to assist the homeless, hard-hit Native American communities, and were about to begin working in underserved nursing homes in Detroit, Michigan.

My interview went well, and I was practically hired on the spot. The team was anxious to bring on an infection control manager with nursing home experience, and they didn't have many prospects. I wasn't surprised, as the workforce specializing in nursing home infection control is minimal and healthcare staff and infection preventionists were already working in facilities or didn't want to go into the field. I was ready. I felt I could make a difference on the frontlines.

I was given an option: support the nursing homes in Detroit or the Navajo Nation. Both were underserved and vulnerable populations, but my main expertise was with nursing homes. As a side note, during my mission in Detroit, I would sign a contract to work as the Havasupai Native American tribe's epidemiologist and later spend over a year helping them remain COVID-19 free.

Within two days of my interview, I was officially hired to work with the Detroit mission. I told them I could go on-site for one month of the three-month mission, which was already several weeks underway.

I had a week to get my medical clearance and other preparations completed, and I was nervous. Detroit was a hot zone, and my job would be to go on-site in nursing homes to contain and mitigate the virus, and to ensure that residents and workers were as protected as possible. This was also during the time of great political unrest with the murder of George Floyd. Protests were being demonstrated nationwide, including downtown Detroit.

The MSF hiring paperwork said that PPE was provided but not guaranteed and that we understood this risk and accepted it. *Whoa! Wait! Hold on!* I was already taking a risk by going into the nursing homes; now they were saying that we might not have PPE? I wasn't willing to do that. When I asked Rogier about this, he said it was simply a formality and that there was, indeed, PPE. With the nursing homes struggling to secure their own supplies, it was imperative that we not use any of their valuable resources.

"I'm not sure," I told my husband, Brian. "It's such a risk. I mean, I could get sick."

As always, he sat quietly listening to my excitement mixed with fear and worry. "You have to go," he said. "This is what you do. You know what to do to protect yourself."

That's all it took. His support was everything.

I got my medical clearance, even with seasonal asthma, and packed for the month. Having spent an entire month in Knoxville recently, I was prepared to pack up again, including my comfy pink polka-dot robe, pillow, and aromatherapy diffuser. I knew that comforts from home during such a challenging time would be necessary, so I let go of the need to travel light. I wasn't entirely sure how our living arrangements would be, but I knew we would be staying at an apartment complex in downtown Detroit. Fitting in and living like the locals has always been the MSF way.

Shannon, the Supplies, Logistics, Administration, and Finance (SLAF) manager, picked me up at the airport. She seemed a bit rough around the edges, a no-nonsense kind of lady, almost military-like. We chatted on the thirty-minute drive from the airport to the apartment, and her continual remarks about how we had it "so good" in Detroit caught me off guard. She referred to our lodgings as super posh, along with our "New York" salaries. She did have a point about the pay: With normal international missions, including physicians' salaries, compensation is around $2,400 per month. I was being paid considerably more, with an additional two weeks of pay for the time I would have to quarantine when I got home. My motivation for providing support was not monetary, although I was happy about the salary as it enabled me to leave my business for the month.

The team and I were lodging at the Detroit City Club Apartments in downtown Detroit. This high-rise apartment complex appeared quite nice on the outside; however, once inside, it reeked of cigarette smoke and marijuana. The common areas, such as the elevator, were quite dirty.

"You'll be sharing a room with Anna," Shannon told me. "This will also serve as the medical office."

I wasn't exactly sure what "the medical office" meant, and I was honestly disappointed that I wasn't assigned a private one-bedroom apartment like many other team members. All in all, I didn't really care. I was here to adapt, roll up my sleeves, and get to work.

When we arrived at the apartment complex, I immediately went to the twenty-third floor to meet the team in the coordinating office in one of the apartments. I met with Heather, the Medical Coordinator overseeing the mission. She was an American from Brussels, roughly my height at five-foot-five, and Italian with long, thick black hair. She was super bubbly and pleasant, and I instantly knew we would get along just fine. I was told over and over again by a vast number of MSF staff interviewing me that having me on board with my expertise was critical, and the team was looking forward to my arrival. I was also repeatedly reminded not to be afraid to offer solutions, as this was a new, underdeveloped project without all the t's crossed and i's dotted.

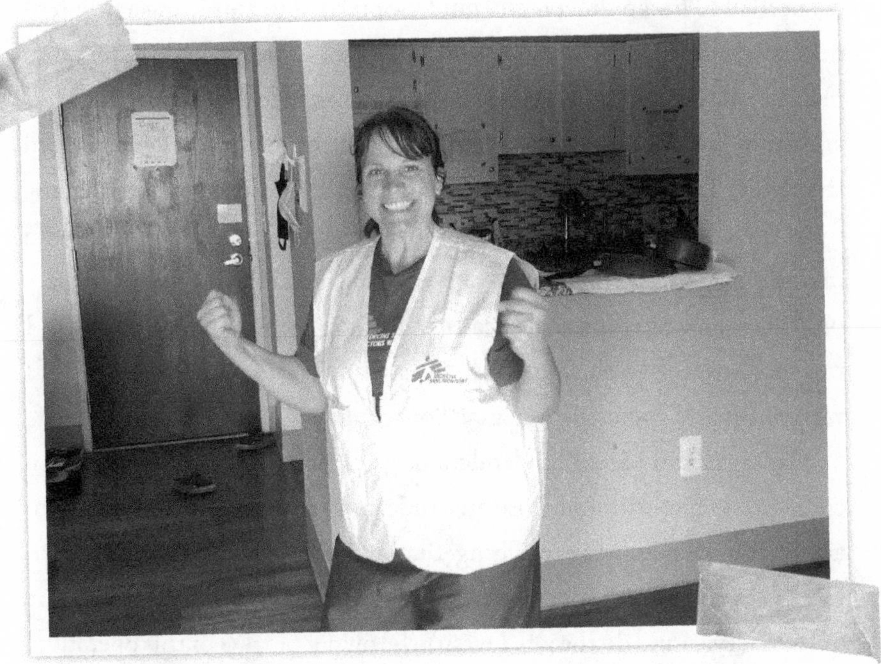

First day with MSF in Detroit, Michigan

I took this to heart and fearlessly set out to bring solutions. Within hours of my arrival, I presented Heather with a printed binder I'd made prior to leaving. This is a tool that my nursing homes back home always appreciated, made up of essential infection control materials such as assessments, evidence-based infection control practices for hand hygiene, EVS (also known as "housekeeping"), and other useful tools like transmission-based precaution signage for the resident's room.

Heather quickly thumbed through my example and then politely said, "Don't you think the nursing homes already have enough resources? Don't you think they're already drowning in paperwork?"

She had a good point, but I knew there were more online resources than most nursing homes knew what to do with, and that was a problem. The online resources were an interconnected spider web of chaos. For example, if I needed to find protocols and guidance related to admitting a new resident to the nursing home, including COVID-19 testing and PPE requirements, it was common to end up down a rabbit hole of information links and never find the answer I was looking for in the first place. I experienced this often. Data on how to care for and combat COVID-19 was coming from the county, state, and federal governments, licensing bureaus, and multiple associations, and much of it was contradictory, leaving healthcare professionals scratching their heads and more confused by the answers. I had more time than the nursing home staff to research questions, and if I was confused, I could only imagine how confused they were.

Having a hard-bound binder detailing best practices was, in my experience, always met with immense gratitude, as it saved the infection preventionist countless hours of searching. But Heather didn't take to the binder. I wasn't in charge of this operation, so I didn't take it personally. I was here to be of service and do the job. I wasn't the owner or CEO of this operation, so I backed off.

I later met Corey, the Water and Sanitation Specialist (WATSAN), a tall and slender man with unmatchable energy. He spent time in Sierra Leone during the Ebola outbreak, along with other members of the team. I was excited to learn from these brave individuals who'd worked on the frontlines in such a dangerous operation. I was the newbie here, and I felt like it. But I was also an expert in long-term care.

The team was pulling from their field experience in Brussels, and I quickly learned that it *would not* work the same in the US. For example, the first on-site visit (at eight in the morning on the second day) I went with Corey and Maria, a medical doctor, and I noticed the nursing home didn't have any alcohol-based hand sanitizing dispensers (known as ABHR). None! I tried to be respectful and listen while I let Corey and Maria lead, but when I couldn't stand it any longer, I made a comment to the nursing home staff that they didn't have any ABHR. How was the staff conducting hand hygiene?

They said, "Well, we have sinks in the resident rooms."

Corey, being so kind and generous, nodded in agreement and said, "Oh, that works! Soap and water are better anyway."

I stood there speechless for a minute then piped up:

"In nursing homes, per CMS, the preferred method for hand hygiene is ABHR in most clinical situations."

It was important to say this because it's a federal requirement, and the facility needed to be made aware of the regulation.[2] In addition, the nursing home was designated as a "COVID-19 hub"; instead of all Michigan nursing homes needing to care for an infected resident, Michigan created "hubs," such as this facility, that were selected by the Michigan Department of Health and Human Services (MDHHS). It was also a brand-new building, only a few months old. I couldn't believe that a new building wasn't created with infection prevention in mind. There were no ABHR dispensers installed, and the facility had carpet which can be difficult to clean and breeds germs. So much for keeping quiet on my first day in the field.

I learned that our basic scope of work consisted of scheduling an on-site nursing home visit with the Michigan Department of Health (they were heavily involved); completing an infection control assessment with the nursing home leadership team, which included an interview and a tour of the facility; providing a report to the nursing home with unique and targeted recommendations for gaps in IPC; and, if needed, scheduling on-site in-service training for hand hygiene and PPE. We also planned to offer wellness support.

This was a solid project; however, it quickly became clear that some nursing homes would need more specific support with repeat visits and to provide one-on-one IPC training.

Maria, with whom Corey and I had been working, left within a day of my arrival, and Karin (a French woman from Seattle) took her place. She was slightly taller than I and slender, with long grayish-brown hair pulled back in a ponytail and a warm smile. She had come from Seattle, where she'd been co-coordinating the COVID-19 homeless response for King County Public Health. Before that, she'd been in Hong Kong with MSF working on the COVID-19 response. I was excited to meet her. I love speaking French, and I love French people.

When I arrived at her apartment, Karin was on the phone, talking quickly and animatedly. She sounded annoyed. I suddenly felt intimidated. I later learned that she was fighting with the New York office for more staff and support. She hadn't been on-site yet but already knew what we were facing and what resources were needed.

A bit later, Karin went with me and Corey to a nursing home. During the drive, we were chatting nonstop (so much for intimidation). I told her I was concerned with the quota that MSF wanted us to meet, around three hundred nursing home visits, when it was possible that some of them would need more support than others. Karin completely agreed. She also liked my idea of having a printed resource binder with the essential training materials that we could provide to the nursing homes.

I was happy to have her as an ally.

It was Karin who named the most under-resourced and challenged nursing homes as "special flowers." We knew our original scope of work with the IPC assessment and report might not be sufficient in making a difference in these "special flowers." Thankfully, the team was open to the concept of "embedding," where we devoted more one-on-one time with facilities that genuinely needed more assistance. It was more important to offer quality services versus simply meeting a quota.

Dr. Buffy and Karin, MSF Nurse Manager

Karin and I spent a solid week creating a robust IPC report template and the process that could be used and modified for all of our nursing homes. Of course, each nursing home would have unique recommendations based on their needs; however, the template would also include basic IPC practices that all facilities could benefit from, such as the best way to dispose of COVID-19 waste. We had Shannon obtain over one hundred half-inch, three-ring binders for us and took one afternoon printing thousands of pages for the IPC binders.

* * *

My journal entries from this time really tell the story.

> Day 1: I went into a nursing home hub. It has the capacity to hold sixty-six COVID-19 positive residents, there were twenty-six. Beautiful building, but no hand hygiene dispensers and carpet everywhere. The staff was constantly touching their faces with their masks on.
>
> Day 2: Went into nursing home today. It was a hot mess. Five positive residents. One positive resident was rooming with a negative resident because there was nowhere else to put them. There are no hand-sanitizing dispensers. They hardly have any PPE. They have had one employee die from COVID. My heart is broken.
>
> Day 3: Another nursing home, but they didn't know we were coming, so we didn't do the assessment. I feel bad for these places because the State is always showing up unannounced, and so they think "we" are the State. I hate seeing people on guard and worried. We are just here to help.
>
> I spoke with CINTAS today and, thankfully, Aaron is a true champion and is going to collect some donations for our team, such

as cleaning supplies. It's pretty unbelievable that a worldwide humanitarian organization like MSF has a hard time getting supplies. It puts everything into perspective. I mean, how can I expect a small nursing home to get PPE when a global leader has trouble? I did, however, get scolded by Shannon for getting the supplies.

I was talking to Corey, the WATSAN, and he was saying he was having a hard time getting supplies, and so I chimed in and offered to help. "Sure!" he said. "Hey, if you can get us supplies, go for it." Three days later, we had supplies.

"MSF works differently," Shannon told me. "We can't just accept supplies from anyone. There is a process to go through."

"Sure, sure," I said. This made sense.

Ah, heck. I'm surprised I found my way into trouble after only three days. I'm working hard to get this mission up and running.

Day 4: Two nursing homes today. One was needing help, although they didn't think so, and the other one didn't need any help. In fact, they were doing so well that they were giving us hand sanitizer. I am a bit annoyed that we were recommended by the state health department to go to this facility. They should only be sending us to facilities that absolutely need our help.

Day 12: My heart aches over the disparity I see. I saw mass testing occur today. We show up to help the facility and conduct our infection control assessment, and the state shows up to test all of their residents (COVID-19 testing) at the same time. There was a CMS memo last week saying the state health departments were assisting nursing homes with the testing process. This is a good thing. What made me want to blow my stack was seeing the health department staff come on-site with full, head-to-toe PPE on. They had hazmat suites and PAPRs, fully decked out. Well, of course, we want our health department staff protected! What about our nursing home staff? Such inequality.

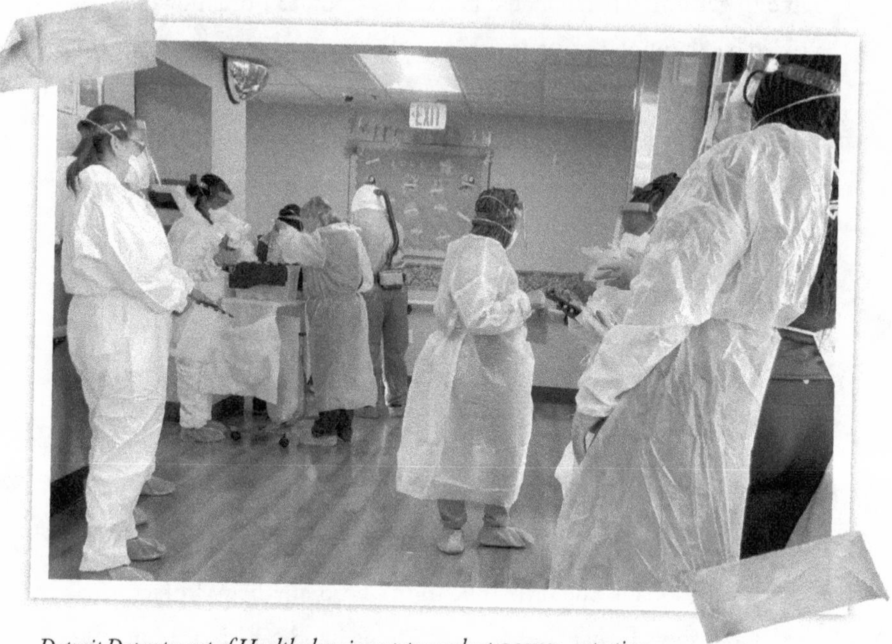

Detroit Department of Health showing up to conduct COVID-19 testing

* * *

The embedding sessions consisted mostly of me working with the housekeeping and nursing aide staff. They simply did not have adequate IPC training, and this was evident.

On one of these visits, I met a housekeeper, Ms. Phyllis, a feisty, no-nonsense African American in her sixties. I asked her to show me her normal process for cleaning the resident's room. Without missing a beat, she walked straight into a COVID-positive room without wearing any PPE. Reacting with haste, I called her out of the room and explained that she needed proper protection every time she went into a COVID-positive room.

Now, I felt scared the first time I walked into a COVID-positive room—even wearing proper PPE. I knew without a doubt that I was putting myself at risk of this disease. Yet somehow Ms. Phyllis did not understand the gravity of this situation.

This was our baseline, this is where the training began. I described how the virus spread through droplets and in the air and then described how Ms. Phyllis could protect herself with conducting hand hygiene and wearing the proper PPE. Given there were no hand sanitizing dispensers inside or outside of the resident rooms, this became our first action item. Obtain hand sanitizer. I had a few extra travel-size hand sanitizers with me, so I gave one to Ms. Phyllis and told her that I would speak to the Administrator about getting more.

Next, I demonstrated how to properly put on (don) the gloves, gown, eye protection, and mask.

Now that we were protected, I asked Ms. Phyllis to demonstrate how she cleaned the room. She first started with the restroom, then, without changing her gloves or getting a fresh cleaning rag, she went straight into the resident's room to clean items like the bedside table.

Inside my mind, I was freaking out because I knew this inappropriate process was contaminating the environment, yet I could not let Ms. Phyllis see my distress. I was here for non-punitive teaching, and the last thing I wanted to do was come across with harshness. With all the calm demeanor I could muster, I gently explained how to clean a room from the "cleanest space to the dirtiest" and the importance of changing soiled rags after cleaning a contaminated or "dirty" area. I then went into the room with Ms. Phyllis and demonstrated what I'd just explained.

At one point, I hesitated to clean the toilet because, quite frankly, I felt overqualified. I almost turned to Ms. Phyllis to have her do it, but then I thought, "You know, she and I are more similar than we are different." I cleaned the toilet and showed her the appropriate manner in which to do it.

I wish I could say that my humility lasted, but it didn't. Later that evening, I found myself joking with the team that I got three college degrees to clean toilets. In my journal later that night, I wrote, "That was so rude and arrogant of me." I am truly honored that I can go into these facilities and help them, whether I'm cleaning the toilets or sitting at the CDC. I go where God sends me. "Speak up for those who cannot speak for themselves, for the rights of all who are destitute. Speak up and judge fairly; defend the rights of the poor and needy" was in my scripture the same exact day.[3] Did I feel that God had His hand all over me and this mission? Absolutely! My job was simply getting out of the way, letting go of my ego, and doing His work.

After my "come to Jesus" moment over the toilet, I devoted the majority of my time with the poorest of poor and the most undertrained staff in the facilities—mostly housekeeping and certified nursing assistants. One younger housekeeper, about twenty years old, had only two rags to clean a unit of about twenty resident rooms. When I asked her if she could get more rags, she said she couldn't.

We went down to the basement and found some white rags that had been neatly folded. When we reached out to get them, the laundry attendant standing there yelled at the housekeeper.

"You know better! These are not for housekeeping! Go over to the bucket and cut up some rags if you want more."

The housekeeper looked at me as if to say, *I told you so.*

We went over to the bucket that was pointed out to us and pulled out some old towels. They were too difficult to cut, and anyway we had no scissors.

"See, Dr. Buffy, this is why I just come in, put my head down and do my job," the young woman told me. "I don't want to cause any trouble."

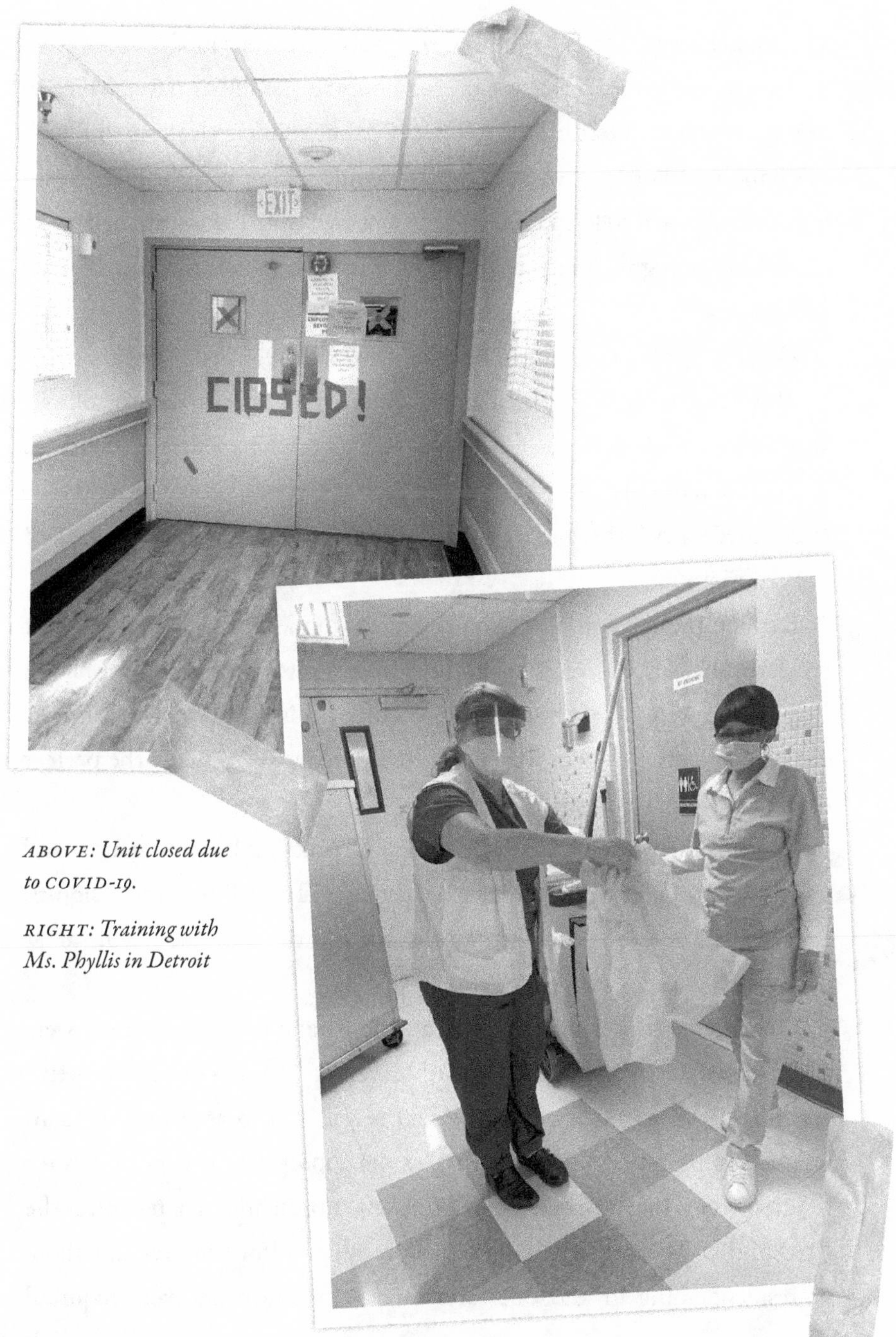

ABOVE: Unit closed due to COVID-19.

RIGHT: Training with Ms. Phyllis in Detroit

"Look, honey," I said. "You need the tools to do your job."

This was frustrating. First, that the housekeeper didn't have a voice to speak up for fear of retribution and second that a simple cleaning tool such as a hand towel or "rag" was not being provided. How was the housekeeping staff supposed to keep the environment free from contaminants?

When I brought this situation to the attention of the administrator, he had no idea.

"We can get her more rags," he said. "That's easy!"

This communication breakdown was system-wide. For example, another housekeeper in the facility was using brown paper towels to clean.

Fortunately, CINTAS had donated over two thousand orange and blue microfiber washcloths, and on subsequent visits, I brought them a stack of sixty or more.

Early in the mission, our team began to wonder if we came to Detroit too late. In fact, one nursing home administrator told us, point-blank, "I wish you were here a month ago." Had we missed the storm? I finally decided that even though we came a little late, it was actually the perfect time for MSF to be on the ground.

What I noticed, week after week, was IPC practices becoming more and more lax. The crisis was over, or so we thought. Two to three more significant waves would hit Michigan afterward, and the staff had begun to let down their guard.

One administrator told me that he knew hand hygiene practices were going down because he had only three empty hand sanitizer dispensers, where the previous month he had seven. It also appeared the staff was becoming lax and not adhering to the appropriate IPC protocols for residents on a fourteen-day quarantine. As a precautionary measure, the CDC and CMS required that any new resident admission, re-admission, or resident going in and out for medical appointments were required to remain quarantined for fourteen days in their room, with their door closed, on droplet and contact precautions (with gown, gloves, mask, and eye protection).[4]

We observed several facilities where the staff was not wearing the appropriate PPE when walking in and out of the rooms; improper signage indicating this requirement; and residents leaving their rooms to mingle. It quickly became apparent that even though we didn't come during their initial outbreak, our expertise and assistance were still much needed.

More than anything, I observed that staff needed mental health support to recover from the pandemic-induced trauma experienced in April 2020. They saw dozens of their residents, staff, and even family members get sick and die from COVID-19. They'd operated while incredibly short-staffed, had state surveyors on their back, little to no resources, and minimal initial COVID-19 testing capabilities. These facilities were on the frontlines of a war without armor or weapons, with confusing and contradictory orders to carry out. They were sitting ducks and paid a high price. They were vilified on the news and treated with contempt and disregard.

Fortunately, nearly six weeks from the inception of the project, our psychologist was able to gain entrance into the nursing homes during our initial on-site assessment, and while we conducted embeddings and in-service trainings. She started connecting with the staff that needed support and resources. Only a psychologist can speak to this, but I believe there is much work that needs to be done in the mental health area, as there are few resources to choose from, especially in-person counseling.

About mid-way through June, Marybeth Wargo, a nurse practitioner with more than ten years of nursing expertise, a bachelor's in nursing and a master's certificate in public health, joined our team as the nurse manager—a vital role in our mission. Prior to COVID-19, Marybeth had spent time overseas working in refugee camps in Syria, Mali, the Central

African Republic, and Ethiopia on the border with South Sudan, conducting contact tracing for hepatitis B, measles, and whooping cough outbreaks—infectious diseases that are highly transmissible in a community.

Marybeth had little experience working directly in long-term care facilities, but what she experienced working on the frontlines in an underserved New York hospital prepared her for diminished resources and undertrained staff within nursing homes. In March 2020, she worked on the frontlines when everything with COVID-19 was still relatively unknown. The hospital where she was employed served as a safety net hospital in an extremely poor neighborhood—a facility where the highest percentage of patients can't afford care, and either have Medicaid or no insurance at all.

The hospital is an accredited geriatric center, given how many nursing homes surround it and feed into the institution. Most of the patients who came to the hospital in the first month of the pandemic were from the nursing homes; however, the care they received was nearly nonexistent because resources (at the nursing home) arrived too late.

Marybeth vividly described the situation:

> What [patients] we had from the nursing homes were DOA (dead on arrival), and we turned many others away. The hospital I worked at looked nothing like the hospital that my friends were at during their travel contracts. We had beds lining the hallway in the emergency room. We had two people in each bay. All the nursing stations were crowded with patients. There was no dignity and no privacy provided. We had eighty patients on my first day with only four nurses. That's a twenty-to-one ratio of patient to staff, and some of them were on a ventilator.
>
> We had a line of ambulances two blocks long outside of the hospital. That's what a crisis looks like. The nursing homes couldn't get

> the patients to us fast enough, and we couldn't do anything once the patients arrived.

Part of the problem, Marybeth explained, is how systemically flawed our healthcare system is in poorer zip codes. There are fewer resources available when an impoverished nursing home sends patients to a poverty-stricken hospital. She continued,

> I had never been to a hospital like the one in New York. Even on a good day, I was surprised at the lack of quality and availability of resources compared to the Pittsburgh hospital I worked in as a nursing student. I had been in a very old hospital in Pittsburgh, and nothing compared to what I saw in New York. There was no way nursing homes could pass any basic safety regulations if that's what the hospitals looked like around them.

The last day Marybeth worked at that New York hospital, she recalled moving a shelf out of the way of other supplies and foot traffic. Hidden behind the shelf was the Emergency Plan created after the September 11 tragedy. In it was a mass casualty plan, which specifically stated they were to treat only four emergency patients at a time. They couldn't have been further from that plan with their current twenty-to-one ratio.

Marybeth did not want the New York mission to be the end of her COVID story, knowing there were more profound issues occurring within the community. She knew COVID-19 didn't start in the hospital, and having a background in public health and community health, she understood that MSF needed to be in the middle of the crisis work in the US.

> I believed in the project in Detroit, and an asset was getting you on the team, Buffy. I think more help from an organizational level should

have occurred. The place for MSF was in the community. It was in nursing homes. You can still see it today. People haven't stepped in, and the nursing homes are still in positions where IPC is way below the standard it needs to have to provide care with dignity and respect. That's not how our healthcare system should treat people.

When Marybeth came on-site, I was eager to work with her. I was getting ready to depart in about ten days and desperately needed a replacement. Seeing the tragedy day after day, multiple times a day in the nursing homes was taking a toll. At the same time, I saw the COVID rates in my hometown of Phoenix, Arizona, start to climb exponentially. At first, I thought, *What the hell? Did I go to the wrong place? Should I have stayed home?* It made sense that COVID numbers would rise as the temperature was over 110 degrees in the heat of the summer. Everyone went indoors where the virus loves to spread.

I felt the pull of home and was glad to know that Marybeth could step in. But when she did so, our mission was another shock to her:

> Because I had been in the hell that was New York during the first month of the pandemic, with zero PPE or equipment and an overworked staff, I arrived assuming Detroit would still be in that situation. I'd heard how bad the nursing home situation was and knew what was happening was awful, but it looked different than I was expecting. It should have looked like a temporary emergency. Instead, it was a long, chronic catastrophe. The problem was much deeper than what was happening during the first month in New York.
>
> Part of the difference between New York and Detroit was seeing people initially react in a one-month panic mode, trying to do everything to protect themselves and taking extra care to be a lot more careful. By

the time I got to Detroit in June, people were tired of COVID. They were exhausted by daily changes to protocol, worn out by not having the support they needed. It felt, especially in the poor, lower-income nursing homes, that they were completely forgotten. That, combined with the chronic nature of the situation, created a greater crisis than in New York, which was a crisis dealing with a fast-paced change. In Detroit, it was a matter of being ignored forever and never having been provided a list of clear protocols.

I think we arrived at a point in Detroit where people were exhausted by COVID from working through the thick of it. They were burned out.

Marybeth soon found the beauty of working in the nursing homes with the one-on-one support that MSF offered to their facilities.

"We were there working hand-in-hand with them," she continued. "So many people told us nobody had ever taken the time to explain processes and requirements. There were several nursing homes where we were told they didn't have training for infection control."

After being on-site in dozens of nursing homes, I completed my mission with Detroit at the end of June that year. I'd been asked to continue, but calls for help were coming in at an even greater rate from other locations. I needed to leave my footprint and move on to the next job. Arizona now had the highest COVID-19 positivity rates in the world.

My mother-in-law Linda knew what I had been doing and was kind enough to pay for a weekend stay at a resort when I arrived back in Arizona. I knew I needed at least a few days to decompress from the constant stress of being on-site and the complete powerlessness I frequently felt. Brian was anxious to see me, but I had just been to "war" and needed a few moments to gather myself. Being the kind man that he is, he completely understood why I didn't go home first. In fact, he picked me up from the airport and brought me to the hotel. It was wonderful and luxurious, but I felt guilty. The nursing home staff wasn't taking a break, and neither were the residents. Although my family and friends were begging me to rest, and while I was physically relieved, it was much harder to shut off the memories of the crisis and my colleagues' place in it.

MSF Detroit team (left to right): Dr. Buffy, Heather, Ella, Corey, Karin, Anna, Marybeth, and Shannon

After being there for twenty-four hours, Brian came to the hotel. I broke down and started sobbing. I sat on the oversized back patio that overlooked a beautiful lush green golf course, bright blue sky, and the Pinnacle Peak mountains in the backdrop. All was serene and quiet. I had my favorite coffee mug that said, "My Favorite People Call Me Nana," and my journal on the coffee table for releasing my thoughts. I was mad, sad, and traumatized. It didn't seem fair. None of it. The lack of PPE, the lack of support, the state coming on-site dressed head to toe protected while the nursing homes made do with scraps. In what world did any of this make sense?

Brian consoled me, reminding me that my efforts did matter and were important. Still, I felt small and insignificant, being acutely aware of the distress that was occurring in an industry in need of repair.

I'd checked into the resort on Saturday, June 27, and on Tuesday, June 30, a nursing home in southern Arizona contacted me about a terrible COVID outbreak. They were one of my clients and had more than twenty residents test positive for COVID. The staff was panicked. Not even pausing to think about it, I told the administrator I was on my way. My bags were still packed from Detroit, so I put them in the car and made the nearly four-hour drive south. I was glad to come on-site and help the facility, where I quickly learned that they were reusing PPE incorrectly, thereby putting themselves at risk for contamination.

I made a grave mistake that day.

The entrance to the COVID unit was through one door from the outside of the building. I went inside. There was a PPE bin at the front entrance, and I opened the PPE drawer to find a long, white folded paper gown. I opened it up, and to my dismay, found the type of paper gown used for patients during a medical exam. They were patient gowns that did not provide a water barrier, cover the arms or tie to fit the body. Unaware that this gown didn't provide protection, the facility had purchased ten cases of them.

While talking to the staff, I observed one of the CNAs putting on used PPE in a way that could contaminate her. In my own panic to protect the healthcare worker, I said, "Hold on. This is how we have to don used PPE."

I took my face shield and N95 respirator off right there, to demonstrate the proper way to don the PPE.

Shit! What the hell was I thinking? I am on this positive unit and just took off my protection!

Clearly, I wasn't thinking straight. I gathered myself, hoping the staff wouldn't notice my grave error, and continued with the assessment.

I encouraged the staff to hang up their reusable gowns in such a way that the outside "contaminated" side would hang on a hook facing the wall and the clean "inside" would face out so the staff could easily slip their arms into the "clean" uncontaminated sleeves. Think of how you would hang a coat on a coat hanger and do it the complete opposite way with the inside of the coat facing the outside. This was considered the "cleaner" side of the PPE.

I went on to remind the staff to use the hand sanitizer every time they went into a resident room and not to wear gloves in the hallway, their common practice, because if they were wearing gloves in the hallway, then they weren't washing their hands.

I worked with the facility on-site for two long days. After hours, I would start the process of responding to the dozens of emails that awaited me. In addition, I had made a prior commitment to conduct a virtual presentation for the national AHCA conference on best infection control practices. It appeared as though every minute of my time was accounted for. Luckily, I was able to record the training via Zoom and sent it off to be presented nationally at a later date.

My plan was to go on-site for the third day; however, during the night, I felt body aches and chills.

Shit, I thought. *I've got it now.* Knowing that I had an almost four-hour drive back to Phoenix, I called the facility administrator, letting him know that I didn't feel well, and drove home. I went to urgent care that day for a COVID test.

To this day, I still haven't received the results from that test.

It turns out COVID-19 wasn't the only health risk I was facing. Like many healthcare professionals, an incredible amount of stress was silently building inside me as I moved from one scenario to the next. My body dealt with this buildup on its own schedule, on its own terms, without warning.

Several days after returning home from the site visit in southern Arizona, I was resting on the couch at home watching a movie, and suddenly I had an excruciating pain radiate up my neck into my head. I was immediately in the worse pain I'd ever experienced and began vomiting.

Brian called the paramedics.

The paramedics came in and were able to get me onto a gurney. They asked my husband if I'd ever had a migraine. He told them yes, but not like this.

They started an IV and pushed morphine.

No relief.

They gave me a barf bucket to hold onto and wheeled me out. I don't remember getting in the elevator or leaving the building. I do remember a woman firefighter saying she was going to go with me. Brian could not go because hospitals were not allowing visitors.

At the hospital, I was taken for a CT scan. I couldn't stop throwing up, and the pain was excruciating—it took nearly four hours to get my pain under control, and the nausea lasted twelve hours.

The results of the CT scan? Clear.

I must have finally relaxed after five weeks of intensity and trauma, dumping all the tension that I had been holding onto in my body.

The doctors wanted to keep me overnight on the telemetry floor because they saw some fluttering on my EKG and wanted to monitor me. I also was given a rapid COVID-19 test. The results were negative.

The next day the neurologist came in and said, "You had a severe migraine...here, take this pill if it happens again...blah, blah, blah...have a nice day."

The cardiologist said, "We thought we saw A-fib on your heart strips; it wasn't, but there was some heart fluttering, so I'm going to have you wear a heart monitor for thirty days to see if anything is going on. Now, get the hell out of here! COVID is taking over this hospital. You're young and healthy. Go!"

I wore the heart monitor for ten days and had an allergic reaction to the sticky component. I sent it in any way and was told that I had some heart fluttering, probably from too much stress and drinking too much caffeine.

My body had hit a hard brick wall. It was only July, and this pandemic had only begun. I knew my work wasn't complete. From that point, I knew I had to prioritize my physical health. If I were going to be effective and stay healthy, I would have to deliberately eat right, exercise, and rest.

In my journaling and in conversations with friends and family, I'd been saying things like "My heart is so broken" and "It's breaking my heart." I knew I needed to stop using that phrase and say instead, "My heart is strong!"

CHAPTER 7

DOCTORS WITHOUT BORDERS: HOUSTON

"Until recently we've chosen as a society not to really see nursing homes until we need them.... In their current state, they're overregulated, underfunded, and have low social respect."
—Terry Fulmer, President John A. Hartford Foundation

Around mid-July 2020, MSF recruiter Rogier contacted me and asked if I'd be interested in joining the MSF nursing home team if they moved their next mission to Arizona. COVID-19 rates were sky high in the state, hovering around 30 percent positivity, meaning that for everyone who tested for COVID-19, about a third came out positive. In the end, the MSF epidemiologists determined that the Houston, Texas, nursing homes were more in need than those in Phoenix.

I was busier than ever with local work, but I wanted to support the new team. I let Rogier know I could come on-site for one week. I'd already made plans to visit Katie and my grandson Adrian, in Knoxville, Tennessee, so my start date in Houston had to wait until August 31.

Around the same time, I was getting phone calls and emails nearly every day from nursing homes that had to complete a CMS-2567 directed plan of correction (DPOC) as the result of a state survey. A CMS-2567 is a federal form that indicates non-compliant practices from a healthcare provider such as a hospital or nursing home.[1] The DPOC is a written plan in response to the deficient practices and includes how the facility is going to remediate the infractions.[2] I received more calls in a few weeks than I had in years.

What the heck was going on? I wondered.

A few days before I left for Tennessee, I received a phone call from a nursing home in Idaho that was required to have an infection control consultant come on-site weekly for two months, followed by a monthly schedule for four months as part of their DPOC. I had never seen such a strict CMS-2567. Typically, the DPOC work can be completed remotely, which includes assisting the nursing home with a root cause analysis, educating the staff, and completing a performance improvement project (PIP).

They must have done something really bad, I thought, *to have the state require them to have an IP come on-site for a total of six months.* I didn't see how this could possibly fit into my schedule but thought if I went on-site every other Friday, stayed the weekend, and went on-site again on Monday (counting as two separate weeks), then it just might work.

It took quite a significant amount of rearranging to fit this nursing home into my schedule as I was juggling multiple projects. I was supporting the Havasupai Native American Tribal community remain COVID-19 free, working on a new Arizona State Nursing Home Emergency Preparedness grant that was supporting all Arizona nursing homes, conducting on-site visits, and helping prior nursing home clients navigate the reopening of their facility to visitors, all in the midst of climbing COVID-19 rates. The cry for help was enormous, and the workforce was scarce.

Brian and I flew to Nashville and were quarantined in Chattanooga for four days. We took the weekend off for hiking and kayaking, and the rest of time was spent working remotely with my clients.

While Katie and her husband took a few much-needed days away, we enjoyed three-month-old Adrian, who was starting to smile and made the cutest baby noises. Sadly, to fit the MSF mission into my schedule as well as the commitment in Idaho, I had to cut my time short with Katie and her family. I left for Houston the following week.

I was nervous going back out with MSF, as the Detroit mission had been so taxing. *How was I going to be able to do it all?* I wondered. The MSF nursing home mission was a continuation from Detroit, so at least I knew what I was stepping into. And nothing had to be created from scratch; the playbook was written and being implemented in a new city.

Marybeth had completed the Detroit mission and helped get the Houston team settled in. She left days before I would arrive, anxious to get to her sweetheart in Germany. COVID had thwarted her original plans of reuniting with him since Germany (and most other countries) only allowed essential workers inside. The world was being especially cautious with the US, as our COVID-19 rates were out of control, disrupting society and causing heated political movements. Somehow, Marybeth managed to get into Germany and reunite with him, and days later, I received a WhatsApp picture of her wearing an engagement ring.

I was briefed by Marybeth that the Houston team was much more relaxed and took evenings to eat together, ensuring there was an appropriate balance of work and rest. That had been my biggest challenge in Detroit; we'd worked eighteen-hour days—not a sustainable pace. She also told me that unfortunately, the nursing homes were more resistant to MSF's help in Houston. Why the nursing homes wouldn't take any help they could get always baffled me. They may have assumed that the help we offered basically amounted to intimidating strangers giving them orders in their building. Even though our support was focused on working together with the facilities to listen to their challenges and solve problems together, without knowing this, their fears were valid.

Rebecca, the SLAF, picked me up from the Houston airport. She was tall, slender, had red hair, and tons of energy. A lover of singing, dancing, and documentaries, Rebecca later coerced the team into watching a horrifically terrifying documentary about clowns. We had a lively forty-five-minute conversation from the airport to the hotel.

We were housed at the Marriott Towns Place, an apartment-style hotel. I had my own room, which brought an added layer of comfort. When we arrived, the team was gathered at the hotel's outdoor patio, ready to have dinner. I checked in at the front desk, got the key, put my bags in the room, and went outdoors to meet the team. The weather was typical for Houston in August: muggy and humid. Marybeth had already departed, so everyone else was new to the nursing home work. I met Kira, the nurse manager; Audrey, the MEDREF; and Whitney, the MSF coordinator who was tall, bald, and had a well-groomed beard he combed with his hands.

There was an array of Mexican food on the table that Whitney had picked up from Pollo Loco. "Please, help yourself," he said.

I wasn't as hungry as I was anxious to jump in and get to know the team. They had received all of the training videos and materials we'd developed from Detroit, along with Marybeth's instructions, but still felt more training was needed. That's why I was there.

Whitney was earnest and concerned about the lack of "buy-in" from the community. He felt that the team wasn't getting adequate support from the public health and advocacy groups to get us into the nursing homes. In fact, one of the largest national nursing home advocacy groups told MSF they weren't needed—there were already too many groups coming in to help the nursing homes. I could tell that Whitney was incredibly stressed by the resistance. Obviously, MSF was paying a lot of money to have this team here, and if we couldn't get into the nursing homes, it would be a problem. I reassured the team that Detroit had been in a similar situation; it could take time to get buy-in and earn the trust of the nursing homes.

What I would soon discover was that a new wave of state and federal surveyors were coming on-site and contributing to the nursing homes' reluctance for additional help. The surveyors came in with a "COVID-19 targeted IPC checklist," and if they identified any deficient practices, they would follow up with punitive action. It's no wonder the facilities were wary of strangers in the building.

After going to a few nursing homes, I noticed their chief complaint wasn't necessarily COVID-19 but how the state and federal surveyors kept making multiple visits to hand out citations they felt were nitpicky. I was also being told that nursing homes were utterly confused by the COVID-19 guidance and which agency's guidelines they were supposed to follow since the county, state, and federal guidance was often contradictory.

One nursing home's property lines were actually across two different counties, but they were required to report to both counties, each with different guidelines and requirements. The rule was to follow the most stringent guidance; however, it was nearly impossible to keep track of the ever-constant changes and to know which were the most stringent.

I had one administrator tell me they had guidance from the state asking them to educate their staff about new requirements at ten in the morning, only to have it completely changed by three in the afternoon the same day. The changing guidelines combined with the strict standards to which the surveyors held the nursing homes created undeniable stress with both leadership and staff.

We found that employees were so confused they were doing ridiculous things. One facility was isolating its residents for thirty days versus the recommended fourteen. When we asked them why, their response was, "We're being extra cautious."

The nursing homes in Texas weren't the only ones in trouble. In a *New York Times* editorial titled "This Is Why Nursing Homes Failed So Badly," E. Tammy Kim wrote of a nursing assistant in Montana who worked in a five-star-rated nursing home and was instructed to treat a dead body as though it were still contagious. She was required to "sanitize the body and stuff any orifice full of cotton, spray them with disinfectant, put a mask on them, and put them in a bag."[3] The star rating system became irrelevant during the pandemic. The virus didn't care how many stars a nursing home had, and wreaked havoc on the industry without discrimination.

To demonstrate the confusion further, in early September, the CDC published research describing situations where an individual who tested positive for COVID-19 could continue testing positive for months after recovering, a situation known as "persistent positive."[4] This was an important discovery, as individuals who continually tested positive had to remain in isolation. Of greater importance in healthcare, staff with persistent positives would create shortages that were crushing to the already limited workforce. Once the research demonstrated persistent positive for COVID-19 could continue for up to ninety days, CMS published new COVID-19 testing requirements that explicitly stated *not to test* a resident or healthcare worker for ninety days if they'd already tested positive, since they were no longer considered infectious.[5]

Easy enough and makes sense...right? Not so fast.

The Texas Department of State Health Services was requiring weekly testing of *all* healthcare workers (regardless of prior COVID-19 status) before a nursing home could open for any visitors, while CMS was simultaneously forcing them to open the doors for visitors immediately.[6]

Audrey, the MedRef (medical nurse) on our team, and I spoke with a husband-and-wife team who owned a small nursing home whose greatest complaint was that their residents weren't doing well. Most of their staff had previously had COVID-19, and several were persistently testing positive.

Consequently, because the state was requiring a COVID-19 negative test for all healthcare staff *before* the nursing home could open, this facility was not able to open. They couldn't even do "drive-by" parking lot visits outside.

I was furious, sitting on the couch in the nursing home lobby directly across from the administrators, listening to their grave dilemma. I told them that the CMS testing requirements clearly stated that "staff and residents who have recovered from COVID-19 and are asymptomatic do not need to be retested for COVID-19 within three months after symptom onset.[7]

"Every single one of our residents has lost weight," this administrator told us. We weren't surprised, given that these clients had gone five long months without face-to-face visitations. The residents weren't thriving, yet the nursing home was stuck in a regulatory nightmare. Never mind the science. Never mind the updated guidance from the federal government based on research.

All I could do was reassure this couple that I'd do my damnedest to resolve this ludicrous situation.

But when we later challenged the head of the state licensing division, we were told, "As long as the nursing home documents state that the CMS and CDC guidance is not to test anyone that has been COVID-19 positive in the past ninety days and documents any tests for staff or resident that come back positive, then it is okay to have visitors."

In other words, if the nursing home documented that they were following the CMS and CDC guidance, they would be okay. But when I told the administrators about this, they were cautious and suspicious.

"No way! It only takes one surveyor to say that we went against the guidance, and then they'll give us a citation and fine us. We can't take a chance unless we get it in writing from the state health department."

I said, "If that happens, and you get fined, then you go through the process and refute or file an IDR (informal dispute resolution) complaint."

"There is no such thing as fighting a citation within the state of Texas."

I said, "Of course you can if the surveyor is clearly wrong."

The administrator looked at me like I didn't understand how things worked in Texas. "We don't fight citations here in Texas."

The medical nurse (MEDREF), Audrey, was a super go-getter, and by the time I arrived in Houston, she had been there for two weeks. Audrey is a humble human being. In the few months that I worked with her, she didn't once mention the two years that she spent abroad working in Liberia and Sierra Leone, Africa, on the Ebola response. She was incredibly teachable regarding the nursing home operations; and until I interviewed her for this book, I had no idea that I'd worked side-by-side with someone who had answered the call to serve when few would, putting her life at risk with the highly deadly Ebola virus.

Audrey described the Houston mission as the most unique mission of her career and believed the rest of the team would say the same thing. This is a statement worthy of stopping to take note. These medical professionals had worked in the worst of the worst scenarios, and to think that the situation in Houston was the most "unique" is extraordinary.

She said that she felt like a fish out of water because of the difficulty to gain access to the nursing homes—something she had never encountered anywhere else in the world. The team was ramped up, ready to begin the mission, but then everything came to a screeching halt when they learned that nobody (nursing homes and public health groups) really wanted them there. The team had to learn local protocols and specifically understand the constantly changing nursing home infection prevention and control (IPC) rules.

Audrey recalls,

> It was changing so often. We had to learn the laws around mask-wearing, visitors, and just everything. It was far more government-based than we were used to. Normally we go into a mission and use MSF protocols...like you go in and you have a handbook of what to do, and you do it. Suddenly, we were talking to the government people and asking the department of health for their guidance. It was very interesting from the organization [on the] coordination side. It was a whole new mentality. We had to get ourselves out of the MSF's "we know what to do" mindset because this was new territory.

Fortunately, for the week I was in Houston, we were able to get into the nursing homes. Along with Audrey or Kira, I had one to two site visits daily, including the weekends. Kira was a highly qualified medical professional, a nurse-midwife, and had worked many field missions with MSF that had contributed to her IPC training. She was incredibly compassionate and empathetic and an absolute pleasure to work with.

While on-site at one nursing home, in the "observational unit," we found a pair of hooks on the wall with about ten green disposable gowns stacked on top of each other—all of it potentially contaminated. We learned that the staff had been told to spray down the gowns with a cleaning/disinfectant agent and then hang them up to dry. This is all they had to use for gowns to protect themselves. *Oh boy*, I thought. *What have I stepped into?* Moments like this required empathetic and compassionate responses, not the freak-out response in my head. "I understand," I said. "We need to work on getting you some more PPE and a different process for reusing it, so you do not contaminate yourself." One nurse asked me if I had gowns that she could use, as she didn't want to use the ones hanging up. I reached around and took off my backpack and pulled out two disposable blue gowns. "Here," I said. "It's all that I have."

Later, on the same unit, we found no clear indication of which residents were in isolation. Unbelievably, the staff didn't know either. Some residents had a negative COVID-19 test, while others had only recently gotten off the positive COVID-19 unit. Still others were brand new admissions. Ideally, the only new resident admissions should have been on this observational unit.

I observed one respiratory therapist wearing a mask with an exhalation value, a mask that doesn't protect the environment from the user's droplets. He walked into a resident's room with full PPE on, including a gown and gloves, left the room, and then walked into another room with the same PPE. He did this multiple times. I asked him if he could describe the PPE protocol on this unit. He said he could wear the same PPE in every room. I was witnessing the staff's confusion right before my eyes.

In fact, the correct PPE protocol was simple, yet misunderstood. If staff was working in the COVID-19 positive unit or red zone, they could potentially wear the same PPE while caring for all the residents, minus their gloves—provided that residents all had the same infectious disease, in this case COVID-19.

In the observation or yellow zone (also sometimes referred to as "warm," "admit," or "step-down") unit, PPE had to be changed after every single resident encounter because it was unknown if the resident had COVID-19 or not. So, a new resident admission would go into the observational unit and quarantine for fourteen days (yellow zone) before going into the

ABOVE: "Reusable" PPE storage—contaminated.

RIGHT: Birthday celebration in Houston with Kira (left) and Rebecca (right)

general population (green zone), to assure that the resident didn't develop symptoms or contract COVID-19.

We observed—and staff agreed—that it was much harder working on the observational unit than the COVID-19 unit, because of the need to don and doff PPE before and after entering each resident's room each time.

Housekeeping was another significant issue. Team members and I noticed that workers were using plain water to clean because they didn't have enough disinfectant to last a week. That was the final straw; Kira and I knew we needed to take action beyond providing IPC education. The staff was in harm's way of potentially contaminating themselves with the reuse of the stacked gowns, not understanding how and when to use the PPE, and the lack of supplies to do their job. Workers were worried about getting in trouble, but we reassured them we were there to help and ensure that they got the supplies they needed.

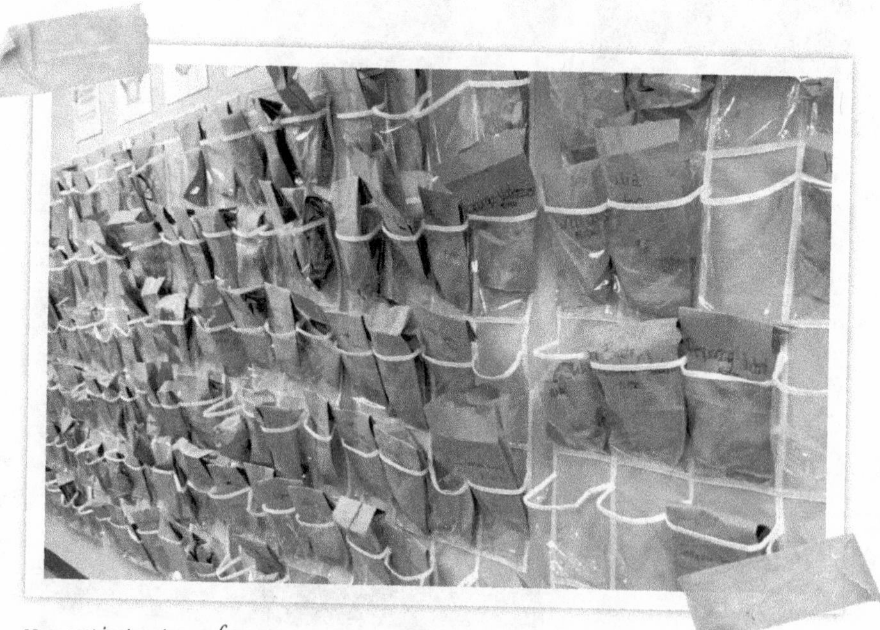

N-95 respirator storage for reuse

When we left the facility, Kira texted the nursing home administrator and let her know about the situation that we encountered, as none of the leadership was on-site during the weekend. The administrator thanked Kira and explained that there were plenty of supplies but that they were locked up. She let us know that she would follow up and verify that the staff got what they needed.

That situation was not exclusive; it was happening in other nursing homes too. It was something that I frequently encounter when I go into a nursing home after hours, on nights and weekends. PPE and other supplies are locked up with no one on-site having access. Therefore, the staff just make do.

The next day, Sunday, Kira and I returned to the facility and had a nice conversation with the nursing home administrator and the regional director. We described the challenges that we encountered and proposed to come back on-site and provide in-service training to the staff, help implement the new processes, and work with the housekeeping staff one-on-one.

Thankfully, this was a facility where the administration was grateful for any assistance that we could provide, as they saw that we were there to help, not point out their flaws as was the custom of the public health authorities.

Word traveled fast among the nursing homes, and our support proved incredibly beneficial, unlike any other support they had ever had. This led to nursing homes becoming more receptive to our work and opening the door to assisting more facilities.

My week in Houston went by incredibly fast—too fast. While I was on-site, MSF hired three local nurses to join our team. Two of them were emergency room nurses, and the other had worked in nursing homes before. They needed training, and the Houston team, still getting their feet wet, asked if there was any possible way for me to come back for one more week.

I agreed to come out for five more days. There was only one stipulation. The only week that would work would be over my birthday, so we would have to celebrate together and eat cake!

I was going nonstop for the entire month of September. I was back and forth to Idaho, having picked up two more nursing homes that were required to have on-site support, and working on remote projects. I had also signed a contract with the Superior Health CMS Quality Improvement Organization (QIO) that supported Minnesota, Wisconsin, and Michigan and was going to start conducting on-site aid for many of their nursing homes beginning in November. CMS had started requiring the QIO's to provide both remote and on-site targeted IPC support for nursing homes with outbreaks. This was a smart move from CMS to provide this type of support; however, the QIO's struggled to get PPE and found it difficult to get trained staff out into the field.

I was working a lot and beginning to feel burned out. Still, I kept going. The day before I left to go back to Houston, I broke down crying.

"I don't think I have it in me to go back out there for another week," I sobbed to Brian. "I'm so tired."

He let me cry. "Just think about the people you are working with," he said, "and how much you love them. But, if you need to take a break, then take a break."

He was right. Working with the MSF team would fuel me as they had the same passion as I did.

I arrived in Houston the evening of Sunday, September 20. The team was occupied, and no one could pick me up, so I took an Uber to the hotel. This was fine with me since I was exhausted and was happy not to engage in a robust conversation.

The following day, Houston got record rain and endured flooding. We were trapped and could not go on-site to any nursing homes. I improvised, conducting remote training with the new nurses. The nurses were engaged and eager to support the nursing homes.

There is often a misconception that any nurse can step in and fill in the gaps for IPC. This simply is not true. The training is specialized and requires extensive knowledge and specific experience. This is especially true in nursing home settings because rules and regulations are far stricter than in hospital settings, and if there is an error in advice, it can cost the nursing home significantly in fines and citations. It was always my recommendation to have a local nurse paired with MSF staff to ensure adherence to appropriate IPC practices.

The Houston nursing homes had many of the same issues as other nursing homes around the country: lack of staffing, lack of training, and confusion about what guidance to follow. They were short on essential supplies like hand sanitizing dispensers, cleaning and disinfecting agents, and PPE. We found that most of the nursing homes had a contract with a third-party environmental services (EVS) company rather than using in-house staff, and it became clear that one of these companies in particular was doing a horrible job. The supplies were subpar, and many nursing homes were being cleaned with fragrances rather than a cleaner/disinfectant agent. Few facilities had any appropriate IPC training in environmental cleaning; therefore, the embedding sessions that put experts alongside staff were critical.

We learned that a common practice for the third-party EVS company was to hang-dry all microfiber towels and mops, claiming it prevented dryer fires. The problem was that they weren't effectively cleaning the towels and mops in the first place. I was working with one housekeeper and picked up a hand towel to demonstrate how to clean a surface and saw black hairs on the towel.

Okay, that's about enough, I thought. *Now we're cleaning with disgusting rags*. I reached out to one of my colleagues specializing in EVS and inquired about this practice of air-drying the rags.

> Hi, I'm flipping my shit. This facility was instructed never to dry their microfiber towels. As we were using them, I noticed how filthy they were even though they claimed they were "clean." I asked how they are laundered and was provided with their policy. Is this ever appropriate? Please help.

The colleague responded with the following:

> That's a stupid policy (can I say that?). It's because they choose crap microfiber that can't be washed at high temperatures. Per the CDC HICPAC 2003 guidelines, drying is an essential part of killing microorganisms. I'd have to see how they manage the formulas, but I would venture to say it's missing many parts of the process to get the rags cleaned hygienically and effectively.

I reached out to the EVS company, a large national organization, to describe what I was seeing. They ignored me. Whitney also reached out and was ignored. We wanted to stress that a healthcare environment required appropriate cleaning and disinfecting to reduce the spread of infectious diseases. A facility should be able to trust that the job is being handled according to the highest standards. Unfortunately, this is an area that needs significant training and improvement.

The MSF team would stay in Houston only two-and-a-half months. Their greatest challenge remained with the nursing homes giving them permission to come on-site.

Audrey explained,

> We were there to improve processes and make things better, and yet half the time, if the state surveyors were there, we'd get kicked out. At one

> building, this happened multiple times. We were constantly shocked that everyone appeared to put everything on hold, even improvement processes and other important things to appease the state or...put on a show. They were so scared of these people. Administrators would say, "No, you can't come in, come back tomorrow," and then just disappear, totally freaked out by the surveyors. The survey process didn't feel like a supportive process, certainly not one to get everyone through a crisis and make things better. It felt more like a scare tactic. It seemed to be confusing everyone.

Audrey would also recall getting hung up on again and again when she'd call to schedule on-site visits.

Why? Why wouldn't everybody accept help from a world-renowned organization known for aid? The reason is deeply rooted in the federal regulatory survey process. What was once originally meant as protection has swung to the opposite extreme through fear and punishment. The process no longer nurtures resident safety. It now prevents true collaboration and assistance from prevailing.

It was a misunderstanding that would haunt me and the teams with whom I worked, time and time again.

CHAPTER 8

STATE AND FEDERAL COVID-19 RESPONSE

"We thought they were here to help, but instead they left us with fifty-four pages of citations."
—Anonymous Infection Preventionist, Detroit, Michigan

As COVID-19 began ravaging nursing homes, the federal government had a tremendous responsibility to step up and provide a coordinated effort to protect the most vulnerable. The national response efforts were confusing and erratic, especially the government position of "enhanced enforcement," which incorrectly assumed an iron fist would ensure that nursing homes provided the highest level of care to their residents.

Every year, a CMS-certified nursing home undergoes a federal survey, a much-anticipated event that can make or break a facility. Every Skilled

Nursing Facility (SNF) is required to comply with "42 CFR Part 483, Subpart B" to receive payments from Medicare and Medicaid, the primary payer for nursing homes.[1] In 2015, CMS paid $55 billion to the industry and covered 62 percent of all nursing home residents.[2]

These facilities are evaluated for compliance by an annual, unannounced state survey. In addition to the state verifying nursing home compliance, they recommend appropriate enforcement actions. Ultimately, it's the CMS regional office that determines if a nursing home is eligible to participate in the Medicare program, "based on the state's certification of compliance and whether a facility has met with civil rights requirements."[3]

A state survey is the greatest source of stress for a nursing home. If the facility is found non-compliant, it can be denied reimbursement for payment or shut down. In March of 2020, CMS announced the suspension of "routine" annual state surveys and an "exclusive focus on immediate jeopardy situations and infection control inspections."[4] Industry leaders would agree these policies were at best premature, and at worst probably dangerous.

By May, about 80 percent of all nursing homes had reported a total of sixty thousand confirmed COVID-19 cases and nearly twenty-six thousand resident and healthcare worker deaths to the CDC's National Healthcare Safety Network (NHSN).[5] Up until this point, nursing homes were not federally mandated to report any infection data to NHSN. Getting them to report at all was an incredible feat, not only for the nursing homes during their COVID-19 crisis but for the small CDC long-term NHSN team.

An early CMS analysis found that one-star quality rated nursing homes were more likely to have larger numbers of COVID-19 cases compared to nursing homes with five-star ratings (ongoing research would ultimately disprove this theory).[6]

In June 2020, CMS issued a press release to nursing homes stating that, in an effort to safeguard the nursing home residents, the Trump

Administration Coronavirus Aid, Relief, and Economic Security (CARES) Act would release funding of $80 million to subsidize the cost to *increase* state surveys.[7] Now I understood why I'd been bombarded with requests to assist so many nursing homes with their CMS 2567 deficiencies. The state surveyors literally pummeled them all at once. Remember, this was occurring in the early months of the "unknown" virus when PPE supplies were low, and staffing was even lower. This was also when the county, state, and federal public health agencies were scrambling to gather information about the virus themselves and figure out the risks involved. It resulted in issuing constantly shifting guidance strategies for nursing homes.

This COVID-19 timeline and nursing homes chart describes the chaotic communications in CMS's and CDC's effort to support nursing homes.[8] Note that despite increased surveys, COVID-19 cases and deaths continued to rise. Early research predicted that as community infection rates went up, so would nursing home rates.[9]

In May of 2020, days before the state surveyors were ordered by CMS to charge full-steam ahead and identify infection control non-compliance, Dr. Konetzka testified before a United States Senate Special Committee on Aging. She explained that the infections and deaths shouldn't be a surprise in nursing homes, given that residents live in close quarters, have comorbidities, and understaffing was a significant challenge exacerbated by the pandemic. She went on to describe other challenges, such as COVID-19 asymptomatic spread (in which a person is infected and contagious with the virus but has no symptoms) and inadequate COVID-19 testing and PPE supplies. Konetzka recommended that funding and technical assistance be provided to nursing homes, so they could hire adequate staffing, essential to reducing the infection risk.

"Under the circumstances, additional resources are critical, including paid sick leave, guaranteed coverage of healthcare costs, and hazard pay for

TIMELINE:

COVID-19 AND NURSING HOMES

AHCA
AMERICAN HEALTH CARE ASSOCIATION

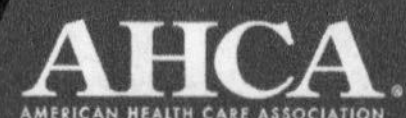

Despite repeated calls for help, nursing homes did not receive resources or priority for months. Even then, the high amount of spread in surrounding communities made it impossible for nursing homes to prevent the virus from entering their facilities. This timeline identifies major regulatory, policy, and resource supports skilled nursing facilities (SNFs) received during the pandemic, as compared to the timing of cases and deaths.

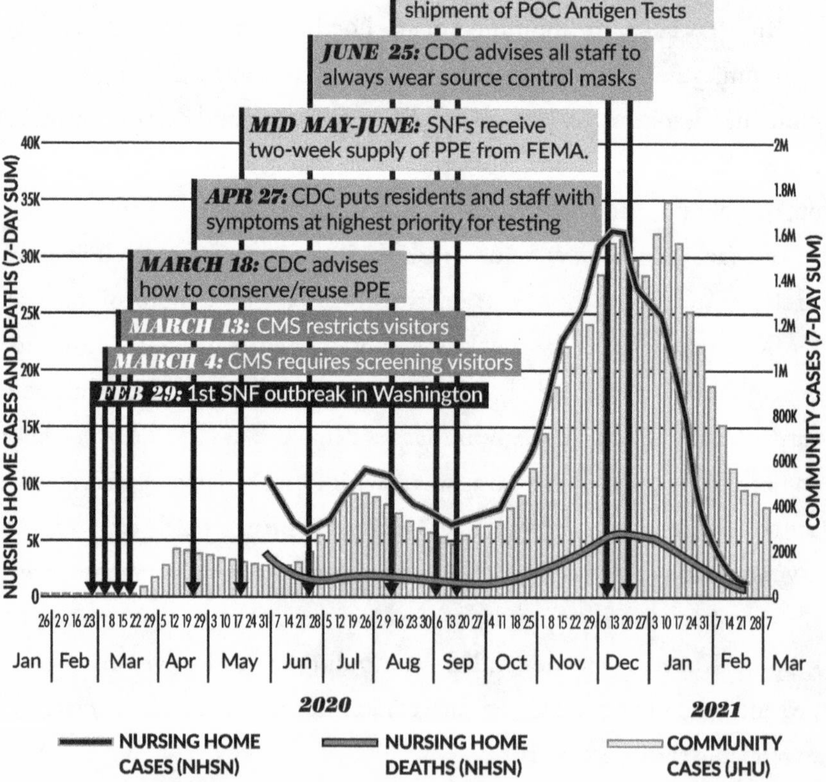

The federal government began collecting and reporting nursing home cases and deaths in May 2020. Since the implementation of the public health emergency, CMS & CDC combined have released fifty-five (or on average at least one per week) major new requirements or guidance in areas of infection control, testing, and PPE use. This does not count minor guidance updates or modifications nor payment changes.

nursing home staff," she said. "Even with these resources, this still may not be sufficient; therefore, surge teams (professionals and experts that work in the facility with the staff) may also be needed to work with the critically ill in nursing homes."[10]

From the beginning, Konetzka felt that policymakers were not treating this pandemic as a cause of nursing home crises but rather some type of quality improvement project. She felt there was ambivalence toward the nursing homes despite her conclusion that we were "in the middle of this pandemic where the research demonstrates that a lot of this [COVID-19] was beyond their [nursing homes'] control."[11]

Policymakers needed to implement consistent public health measures that would control the virus in the community. Instead, there was a dismal failure of policy to be consistent in public health messaging mandates. There was a sense that we could somehow blame the nursing homes even though the virus was raging in our communities outside of the facility. The research showed that the more prevalent the virus was in the community, the more difficult it was to protect the vulnerable. "That has been the biggest disappointment in policy, mostly at the federal level," Konetzka said in an interview with me.

What does all this mean? It simply didn't matter how compliant the nursing home was with quality infection control practices, except with regard to the daily general care and safety usually offered to the residents. If the surrounding community was experiencing high COVID-19 rates, so too would the nursing home. Why? Because the workers lived in the community and came into the facility. The research eventually showed that even the necessary addition of staff would increase the risk of COVID-19 in the facility.

Dr. Konetzka's testimony didn't slow the actions of CMS as they plowed ahead with a plan of allocating $80 million in state and federal funding to conduct surveys rather than COVID infection "surge" teams. That would be like firefighters showing up to your house while it's ablaze, and instead of using water hoses, they'd fine you for faulty sprinkler systems. This, during a time when these particular flames were unlike any ever seen, and the guidance in using your sprinkler systems had been confusing and sometimes impossible to implement. A time when you couldn't get water to fill your sprinkler systems due to supply chain issues. Policymakers were funding the citations instead of the water hoses necessary to put out the flames. It seemed backward—it *was* backward.

The precedent for a punitive federal response began with the first COVID-19 nursing home outbreak in Kirkland, Washington. In a *60 Minutes* exposé, Vice President Nancy Butner described how she ran the Kirkland facility for fourteen years before COVID killed thirty-eight patients and infected sixty-seven members of her staff.

"The virus was in complete control," she said. "It was a guessing game without testing—isolating some and not others, as this was an unprecedented situation. PPE wasn't available, so [staff] bought up oversized men's shirts and wrap-around women's dresses from Walmart. Forty employees, including the Medical director, became sick and could not come to work."[12]

Around that time, the media began assigning culpability for the pandemic. They needed a scapegoat, somewhere to point the finger. I remember watching the news and seeing gurneys of residents, one after another, being transported from Life Care Center. I thought to myself, *My God, these nursing homes aren't prepared.* I saw a disconnect in how the public and media began looking at hospital workers as healthcare heroes while expressing rage at nursing homes. It was heartbreaking. Yet both were subject to the same conditions of inadequate PPE and testing. Governors were embroiled in a bidding war for PPE, and our nursing homes didn't stand a chance.

Dr. Jefferey Duchin, a twenty-two-year veteran of Seattle's King County Health Department, was in charge of the local government response in the Kirkland region. Concerned with the number of residents testing positive, he raised the alarm with the CDC, requesting they send a team of epidemiological disease investigators and lab support, as the facility was down a third of its staff, a common scenario during this and any outbreak. In addition, Nancy wrote a letter to the Department of Health and Human Services, requesting a "strike team" of doctors and nurses to come on-site for support.

When strike teams are deployed, they're to arrive within twenty-four hours. It took the strike team five days to show up, and CMS walked through the door before help arrived. Nancy recalls begging them to leave, as the facility did not have the staffing resources to manage a survey process, one that would take hours and hours away from patient care. The surveyors were aware of their lack of staff and the crisis they were in; however, they insisted on conducting the survey anyway. Nancy even asked the governor to have them leave, but their request was denied. CMS didn't leave, and they didn't offer support.

The surveyors interviewed employees and demanded thousands of documents diverting more than four hundred staff hours away from patient care. The result was a forty-eight-page statement of deficiencies which said that Life Care failed to manage the outbreak, putting residents in immediate jeopardy. To me, this seemed quite plainly like government ensuring responsibility and accountability would not fall on itself. This situation mirrored what happened in countless other facilities.

Seema Verma, the CMS Administrator for the Trump Administration who declined to be interviewed during the *60 Minutes* segment about Kirkland Life Care Center, later tweeted, "You may hear some revisionist history from people who have vested interest in *deflecting responsibility* for the disaster at the Kirkland Life Care nursing home and the tragic deaths in the nation's first COVID-19 outbreak."[13]

Life Care was fined $611,000 by CMS. They appealed both the federal and state actions, and a judge eventually concluded there was no negligence on the side of the facility.

* * *

The first time I went on-site to the Winslow Campus of Care, it was late February 2020. Dawn Weatherbee had heard me present at the Arizona AHCA convention in the summer of 2019 and wanted some support in their infection control program. Like many others, their facility appeared to be doing well, so there was no urgent need to hire my consulting services.

In late February, I received a frantic call from Dawn saying the facility had a scare and thought they had COVID-19 in the building. It had turned out to be a simpler form of coronavirus, not COVID-19 but a common cold.

Still, my services were contracted, and I made the three-hour drive to Northeastern Arizona. Winslow is a small town with a population of slightly under ten thousand; its claim to fame is a reference in the Eagles song "Take it Easy."

Winslow Campus of Care is a 119-bed nursing home that serves a predominately Native American population, and the décor reflects this with beautiful Native blankets and artifacts. My first inspection showed that the facility needed to improve hand hygiene and housekeeping practices. I provided them with resources for free hand sanitizing dispensers, environmental cleaning products, and supplies like microfiber hand towels and mops. When I left, I felt they'd be as prepared as anyone, should they have a COVID outbreak.

I didn't hear much from Dawn over the course of the year. I was on the road, deep in the crisis, and they were working hard to keep COVID-19 at bay. Then on November 20, 2020, I received an email from Winslow's administrator Dan Belisle with news of an outbreak. He asked if I had any advice for them to connect with the director of nurses (DON). I reached out to the DON, but she could not return my call due to the demands of working on the COVID-19 unit. I reached out to Dan by leaving a phone message.

We would both come to regret our inability to connect.

Later, Dan told me:

> I sat here in this office on a Wednesday afternoon, December 9, 2020, in the windy city of Winslow, Arizona. All three of the cities' ambulances were parked in our breezeway. All day the ambulances were coming and going. In and out, in and out. When the final trucks left the parking lot, we could hear the sirens down the road and knew when they reached the hospital. Then there was a pause. An eerie silence.
>
> Next, we heard the swish, swish, swish of the helicopter blades and knew that residents were leaving Winslow Indian Health and being transported to a higher level of care. Each residents' condition was critical, perhaps fatal."

The Winslow facility had been hit with a catastrophic COVID-19 outbreak. Dan said,

> This particular day, I realized COVID-19 was for real. This was huge. I have faced a lot of different adversities in my life, and in general, I am able to hurry, stand up, catch my breath, move on, and think about it later. This was different. The events that transpired this unprecedented day hit me and hit me hard. It was just overwhelming, so overwhelming.

Dan's parents built a nursing home in 1965. It was one of the first skilled nursing facilities in Arizona, created in anticipation of the wonderful financial support coming from Medicare and Medicaid.

Much to the facility's dismay, Medicaid didn't get funded until 1989.

Dan didn't set out to become a nursing home administrator. He graduated from Arizona State University in 1972 and wanted to become a dentist.

"In those days," he told me, "the dental schools only accepted about one hundred applicants per year. If you weren't an A-plus student, you probably weren't going to do it." His mother was a registered nurse and ran the family nursing home; his father, a farmer, would travel back to the Midwest every year to cultivate the crop with his brother.

In the summer of 1972, with Dan's father gone, he helped his mother with the nursing home while he waited to decide his next post-college move. His mother suffered a stroke that summer and became a resident of her own nursing home, spending the last two years of her life a couple of doors down from his office. What started as a one-year commitment for Dan extended into a fifty-year career.

Dan thought perhaps his facility got lucky and would avoid getting COVID-19, as they'd missed the two prior surges in the summer and early fall. But in November, seven residents tested positive for the virus. A week later, they had a total of twenty positive cases. Soon after, multiple staff tested positive, and by December 24, eighty-five residents had COVID-19. A total of forty-two residents passed away.

At the onset of this outbreak, about half of Dan's staff walked off the job as they were terrified of getting COVID-19 and spreading it to their loved ones at home. This left the remaining staff to work sixteen to twenty-hour days, sometimes nineteen to twenty days in a row. Dan and the DON reached out to the state of Arizona and Navajo County several times, asking for help as their work pool dwindled. They were told they could get help for a couple of days and to use the state registry for nurses.

In a small community one hour from the closest urban city of Flagstaff, finding and keeping employees had historically been a challenge. Competing industries pay higher wages with less risk, less burden, and no punitive regulations than those of the long-term healthcare setting.

One of the physicians that was working in the facility during the outbreak ended up in the hospital from the anxiety experienced at work.

"This was a real eye-opener," Dan confided in me. "There are consequences of COVID-19. I don't think I will ever forget the months leading up to it. It reached a point really quickly where it wasn't a question of if it was going to happen, but when it did, would we be prepared? We got through ten months before it exploded all around us. We were hearing about it nationally and thinking, hey, maybe we've dodged it. Probably a little naive on our part, given we were sitting right in the hot spot of the nation."

Two weeks into the outbreak, Dan received a phone call from a state health department infection control specialist, offering to review the facility's infection control practices to see if there were gaps in handling the outbreak. Dan felt initially leery about asking for any advice from the local or state public health departments, which always seemed to be used against him. He talked it over with his DON, and they agreed that the additional virtual help couldn't hurt.

Dan and his DON had a Zoom call with two state infection specialists and three Navajo County public health representatives. They discussed a variety of infection control practices and took a virtual walk through the building with the DON. Dan and his team got some valuable feedback and the specialists told Dan, "Given the circumstances you've got with your physical site and the size of the outbreak, there is not a lot more that could be expected than what you're already doing."

Dan recalled that they were comfortable with what he and his staff were doing, acknowledging that they weren't perfect but were working with what they had.

He knew the report from the public health officials would be submitted to the state health department and that a visit from the state regulatory division would soon follow. Over the years, with stricter state and federal regulations, Dan has seen a shift in the regulatory role. What once was a more collaborative environment has drastically shifted to a punitive one.

"Early on, there wasn't a challenge we didn't stand up to," he told me. "Nowadays, nobody wants to rock the boat." He knew infection control was becoming more of an emphasis since the new federal rule changes in 2016. Still, he considered these requirements similar to the other regulations that had come out in years past, and he began to think of them like biblical commandments: "Thou shalt have an activities director. Thou shalt have a social worker." Infection control seemed like another "Thou shalt" to him.

Back in March 2020, at the onset of the pandemic, Dan recalled a one-hour CMS webinar hosted for all nursing homes. "They were gracious and empathetic; however, the underlying message of the call was 'Don't screw up.' I'm sorry, that was the wrong message, even in March 2020. I mean, God, it would have been a lot easier if the message was, 'We want to be helpful. Here are some thoughts, and what else can we do?' But that wasn't the case."

Dan was correct about his prediction that the state surveyors would come in. "I could see them [surveyors] coming into the building and recalled the conversations with my staff. 'Why don't they come and help us?' they asked."

But help is not what they got. The state surveyors spent a total of three days on-site at Winslow. "I don't think these people were realistic," Dan says. "They were brutally unfair to my nurses, treating them with contempt as if they were incompetent." The surveyors reported that the facility was not substantially compliant, with the serious deficiency at Scope and Severity (S/S) Level J. That meant his nursing home was considered non-compliant with CMS requirements of participation, with violations likely to cause serious injury, harm, impairment, or death to a resident.

As a result, the Centers for Medicare and Medicaid Services (CMS) imposed the following penalties:

- discretionary denial of payment for new admissions effective January 31, 2021, meaning the facility would not receive reimbursement for any new admissions until it was found substantially compliant
- a required Directed Plan of Correction to be provided within ten days of the notice and outlining their remediation plan
- mandatory termination (of payment) effective June 17, 2021, meaning that if the facility didn't remedy the deficiencies, they would no longer be able to receive reimbursement from Medicare and Medicaid residents

Furthermore, CMS imposed Federal Civil Money Penalties for a total of $23,735, stating that if the total amount wasn't received by the due date, a federal interest of 9.625 percent would be added. They explained that if Dan waived his right to a hearing, that penalty would be reduced by 35 percent. Finally, the nurse's aide training program, a critically vital program that kept nursing aides employed in the facility, was prohibited for two years.

While this facility was in a full-blown COVID-19 outbreak and crisis, with nearly half of its staff gone, and after receiving technical assistance from the state and Navajo nation saying they were doing the "best they could," they were cited by CMS for ineffectively utilizing PPE and allowing COVID-19 positive residents to wander the halls. Never mind that nearly 80 percent of all residents at this facility had dementia or other cognitive behavioral issues that would have made isolating them nearly impossible.

While this was going on, I signed up another nursing home in Idaho. Josh Smith, a nursing home administrator from Boise, let me know his building had a pretty good infection control program and hadn't had an infection control tag in the past four years, yet they received an Immediate Jeopardy tag because they didn't have dedicated staff for one resident on the COVID-19 unit.

Calls about IJ tags meant having to move mountains, because of the requirement to have weekly on-site support anywhere from four to eight weeks, then typically bi-weekly, and then monthly. Josh's facility didn't get hit quite as hard as some other Idaho homes and *only* required eight visits.

"I can be there on January 1," I said. I was first on my way to assist two nursing homes in Western Michigan with outbreaks.

As a former Combat Engineer that was deployed to the Al Anbar province of Iraq, Josh was no stranger to stress and crisis. Prior to the pandemic, he was also involved in the Central Idaho Healthcare Coalition, an interdisciplinary collaboration focused on emergency preparedness for emerging infectious diseases.[14] Within this group, they would often talk about what would happen if there was another viral outbreak, using 1918's Spanish Flu as an example to build a response. Would they be ready? They evaluated how they would handle the surge and the response mechanism for interagency cooperation, and how the nursing homes would take the strain off the hospitals. The coalition drew key industry leadership from places such as hospitals, paramedics, and the local health district. In theory, everything appeared to work cohesively, but the reality of COVID was a different story.

When Josh's nursing home had its initial outbreak, it was early in March 2020. They were one of the first facilities hit in Idaho. There was limited testing, but they were doing the best they could at the time.

"It was heart-wrenching to see these people coming up positive, person after person. It really took an emotional toll on everyone," he told me. "We think it was a restorative nurse assistant that brought the virus in, infecting a resident who was a total assist (meaning he required 100 percent support for eating, bathing, and toileting). We made it through but had a really rough go of it."

Another challenge was that some of Josh's staff didn't believe that COVID-19 was real. This was common in many conservative regions of the country. Unfortunately, this belief was demonstrated through actions from the staff, including a nurse in Josh's building who wouldn't wear the PPE the correct way and actually went in and out of resident rooms to deliver medications and dinner trays—literally spreading COVID from resident to resident.

"COVID-19 ripped through the halls like a wild tornado," Josh said. "It was tough. Twenty-two total residents and quite a few more staff tested positive, and two passed away. One resident said, 'This is my home. If I get it, just let me go,' and sadly, his request was honored."

Josh went on,

> Staffing was crazy. Idaho has had significant staffing challenges prior to COVID. It's always a struggle keeping the building staffed appropriately. Then you add ten or fifteen staff members out at a time, nurses, IPs, and staff working the floor. We were spending twenty to $30,000 per month just in incentives to get staff to pick up shifts. People were so tired; they eventually wouldn't even pick up a shift for a five-hundred-dollar bonus. That's crazy! After a while, the money didn't work. It could only take us so far."

In Josh's case, the government had focused on what looked good and not what was best for his facility. "I'll be the first to tell you the importance of having a regulatory environment," he admitted to me. "When you look back on nursing home history, some of the stuff we were doing was barbaric. So, there's a need for a strong set of well-developed rules that we abide by. But the pendulum has swung too far."

During the outbreak, the state surveyors walked into Josh's facility to conduct an infection control survey.

> I was out of the building sick with COVID, working twelve-hour days from home, cocooned in blankets. We had a COVID unit that was well put-together. We have an older building with south-facing windows, and it was hot at seventy-eight degrees, but within the regulatory parameters for the temperature. When you have sick residents, and staff in gowns, and N95 respirators, it's hot and miserable for everyone. So, we put fans in the hall. As a result, we were issued an immediate jeopardy (IJ) for that infraction. When I asked the regulator why we couldn't have a fan, they couldn't give me a reason. We were able to show them that the three air handlers on the unit and in the rest of the facility were under negative pressure, which pulled air out of the halls, not into the halls. This would be appropriate and not increase the risk of spreading an airborne virus. Plus, all of the residents on that hall had a diagnosis of COVID, and if the staff was wearing the appropriate PPE, the chances of it being spread was minimal. In the end, the surveyors cited us on a reference to the linen infection control manual about having fans in the laundry room blowing from clean areas to dirty. We were fined $100,000 in civil monetary penalties.

Josh's corporation decided not to dispute the fines because historically Idaho has a 2 percent chance of overturning citations. If a facility doesn't dispute the citation, then they qualify for a 35 percent reduction in penalties—too good to pass up. Unfortunately, the ramifications of getting an IJ, deserved or not, go beyond the initial fines. The reputation of the facility is damaged, and families of the residents living at the nursing home are more fearful for their loved ones. They're notified that the facility has an infection prevention deficiency of the highest level, one that is "likely to cause serious injury, harm, impairment, or death to a resident."

Josh's nursing home paid $65,000 in fines.

> Imagine what we could have done with $65,000. How many N95 respirators could I buy with that? What would up-grades to the air systems cost? That was with the 35 percent reduction. The state cited us with the IJ prior to leaving our site that day. Our remediation plan was to unplug the fan, and we were done. However, because it was a federal surveyor, we couldn't claim our final compliance until they were done with their offsite review. Consequently, we had IJ-level fines for an additional six days. The fan was immediately unplugged and removed. I don't know if that was worth $65,000. Was the point of that to ensure we had a proper infection control program, or was it a move by the federal government to say, "Hey, we're really cracking down on these heartless providers that are out to suck money out of your loved ones and leave them to rot"? That's the perception of nursing home operators, unfortunately. People believe we just don't care; we don't put the money back into the physical site or the care or training. Maybe some people in the industry have that reputation, but it's just not true. At least not in our building.

Josh remembered when the federal government said they were suspending annual surveys and sending out infection control surveys instead. He recalls thinking, *Okay, is this a collaborative effort so we can get better at our infection control practices, or is this a punitive measure, like "gotcha"?*

The consequences of the IJ were enormous. Josh's leadership team, including himself, the DON, and the staff spent a substantial amount of time on paperwork for regulatory compliance and conducting audits on a process that was already done.

"What would have been better," Josh said, "would have been to have support and collaboration."

The financial implications are harsh, but it goes further than that. This type of punitive environment contributes to increased staff burden, as the attention is taken away from fighting the infectious disease to push paper and conduct busy work to make regulators happy, instead of focusing on what the resident actually need in that moment. In this case, Josh's staff literally worked in fear and questioned their own years of training and experience—this, when all the guidance was unclear, inconsistent, and often impractical.

Sarah, my Northern Arizona client, had described a similar experience with her state surveyors.

"It was not great," she'd said. "We had no government support whatsoever. They just made things harder. I remember we'd get new CMS guidance at ten in the morning, and by two in the afternoon, it was changed. It was a cluster of chaos."

Days after the second COVID-19 outbreak in Sarah's facility, the surveyors showed up before ten in the morning.

> They were not kind, very rude. Shortly into the process, they told me I didn't provide them education on COVID-19 and that they could tag

me. This really threw me off because I figured they work for the government, and they knew about COVID-19. Plus, we had signage and information on the outside of our front door, as well as inside at the reception desk. It felt frivolous.

One surveyor, Sarah found out later, was new.

She was the one who insisted that she go on our COVID-19 unit, so I obviously went in there with her. I tried to get her not to go because we tried to limit anyone from going in for their own protection. I hadn't even gone in there. We used walkie-talkies to communicate between the plastic and with text messages. She [the surveyor] came on the unit with me and had no idea how to put PPE on. It wasn't her playing a game or trying to test me. She really had no clue. She insisted on bringing her clipboard and pen. I tried educating her that we don't take anything in and out, that everything that goes in stays in.

She said, "Well, I need my clipboard."

I said, "Well, you can use a different sheet of paper."

She insisted, "No, I need it for my notes."

So, we went into the unit, and I helped her get all her PPE on. She had nylons on and a skirt, which was really inconvenient trying to put on PPE. We got on the unit, and she talked to the nurse and then was ready to leave the unit. She had no clue to even think about disinfecting her pen and clipboard. I said, "I'll go ahead and disinfect this for you."

She said, "Oh great, that would be nice."

We washed our hands and left the unit. This was during a time that we were already very, very busy and understaffed because of the outbreak, and having to dedicate that many staff members to the surveyors was hard.

In the end, Sarah's facility was written up because one employee was wearing her COVID mask upside down. "It was clear that the surveyor was not a 'let me teach you' person, but a 'let me find something you're doing wrong' person," Sarah said.

After her third outbreak and in fear of the survey process, Sarah always expected a call saying the surveyors were once again on-site.

"You simply pray your staff knows the right answers," she said. "If the staff is wrong, I feel it's on me. If we get hammered, I feel the responsibility."

One important step in passing a survey is having the materials ready for the survey team. Sarah kept a COVID binder, set up how the surveyors liked to see it.

"Because it's proof of everything we have done," she explained. "We spent days making sure that we had everything in a binder for them."

Sarah, like so many of her contemporaries, wishes the government had a more supportive attitude. Instead, she says they come in with fines and tags, and she fears it all.

In August of 2020, CMS issued a press release saying that the government had issued more than $15 million in fines to nursing homes during the pandemic. "We will continue to hold nursing homes accountable," CMS Administrator Seema Verma said, "and work with state and local leaders to protect the vulnerable population."[15]

The average CMS fine was $55,000. Furthermore, state licensing agencies received an additional $397 million (as of April 4, 2021) in federal cash to continue conducting infection control surveys in nursing homes in 2021.[16]

Winslow Campus of Care was one among more than 61,000 focused infection control surveys conducted in 2020, with over 11,500 citations issued for one F-tag alone. The rate of IJ-level findings tripled from 2019.[17]

There was more to come.

CHAPTER 9

GOTCHA!

"This (state survey process) is actually going to kill people. The facilities are not admitting because they are so heavily penalized with survey; therefore, the hospitals will get backed up, and people will die."

—Josh Smith, Administrator

The punitive nature of the regulatory process during the COVID-19 pandemic didn't help those battling the disease in care facilities. An unproductive system that doesn't promote resident safety and is no longer collaborative is a hindrance, not a help.

Often, as I spoke with administrators and researchers, I heard the term "gotcha" used to describe the current regulatory process.

After beginning her academic career in a completely different field, Sylvia switched to healthcare for the practicality, and there she found her calling. She completed her nursing degree at the University of Wisconsin and started working on the orthopedic unit of a local hospital.

Shortly after, she moved to public health and worked with the Nursing Home Association, specifically in home health and hospice. She was glad to get out of the hospital and provide nursing care to patients at the end of their lives.

In Wisconsin, she worked as the unit manager at a nursing home that was, as she put it, "cutting edge and out on the front lines." She moved to Arizona, where she ran a dementia unit, then began consulting in thirteen states, helping nursing homes that needed to get back in regulatory compliance. She is no stranger to the burdens that nursing homes experience.

Growing weary of the travel, Sylvia confined her work to Arizona and worked for the state health department for ten years. She started as a surveyor and then began training other surveyors. As the state Resident Assessment Instrument/Minimum Data Set (MDS) coordinator, she oversaw the whole MDS process and assessment and finally became the program manager or Bureau Chief.

Secretly, I'd hoped I was wrong about my perception and experience with the regulatory agency, that it was just my perception that the chaos surrounding the state and federal survey process during the COVID-19 pandemic was my own misconception. I hoped Sylvia could prove me wrong.

Instead, she described how the surveyor training program has significantly changed over the years and told me that it wasn't nearly as rigorous as in the past. Inadequate training may be a contributing factor to the "gotcha" mentality as the surveyors can't go deep into processes. In the past, requirements of becoming a surveyor included six weeks of rigorous in-person classroom training, an intensive national in-person training program, and a national test. Upon receiving a passing score, the student would then be paired with a mentor for multiple on-site nursing home site visits before they had the opportunity to survey on their own.

The current training is all online. In fact, anyone can go through the training at *qsep.cms.gov*. When I learned of this, I personally signed up for the training to explore its modules.

"They just sit in a cubicle and obtain all of their training online," Sylvia said, "and after they pass a test, they go into the field to conduct surveys. There aren't a lot of mentors."

Just as there is a shortage of healthcare workers in nursing homes, it is also a challenge to find qualified regulatory surveyors. This is part of the reason the education and other prior criteria have softened. Anytime there's a shortage of a necessary position, the barriers to entering that position erode and the qualifications become less stringent. Unlike when Sylvia began her career, today's surveyors don't even have to be nurses. They can be a social worker even though only nurses are supposed to review certain criteria during the survey process, such as physical examination of residents.

"The industry regulations are starting to waiver, given how hard it is to recruit nurses," Sylvia said. "Due to the low wages of the surveyors, they get poached by the nursing homes and hired as executive staff and trainers to help with survey preparedness."

During the COVID-19 pandemic, the loudest complaint I heard from nursing home staffs wasn't the lack of PPE or even having a COVID-19 outbreak. The nursing homes were able to rally and work together to care for the residents in such circumstances. What staff complained about most was the punitive nature of the state and federal surveyors.

"It's about nursing homes being overregulated," Sylvia believed. "Surveyors aren't going into hospitals and conducting surveys during COVID-19, they're not going into dialysis outpatient centers, they're not going into outpatient clinics, they're not going anywhere else. They're going into nursing homes and blaming them for poor COVID-19 outcomes but not looking at the outcomes for other provider types. Nursing homes, in general, were seen as being under-prepared, which was in fact true. But given that infection control has taken a back seat to other quality measures, should it be a surprise that the nursing homes were less prepared? Wouldn't it seem more appropriate to offer them more help?"

Sylvia is right. All CMS annual state surveys were suspended, except for nursing homes, yet COVID-19 targeted surveys continued—which was not the case for any other healthcare provider.

Among those, nursing homes were the least prepared, so a disciplinary process was punishing those already suffering, like punishing the poor because they are already weak instead of providing support and help. It looked like a blame-shifting play meant to point the attention away from the federal response. The government picked the low-hanging fruit, more concerned with assigning fault than the actual safety of its citizens.

The survey process during COVID-19 has made things worse instead of better. Many nursing homes were visited by a minimum of six state or federal surveyors in one year alone, and when problems were found, the thinking was that these facilities still didn't have it right. "So they were going to increase the penalties even more, which is what CMS did," Sylvia said.

"It's just one stick after another—there aren't even carrots anymore. It's so hard when we see some of the best administrators we know literally in tears and wanting to get out of the industry. They can't handle it anymore."

I had seen this very thing in all the nursing homes I'd recently worked in; remembered all the weary, beaten-down nursing staff, sat with administrators and cried, such as the one from Wisconsin on a cold winter day in January 2021, during the third and most severe COVID-19 wave. She'd said, "We lost thirty-eight of our long-term care residents. They were our family too. And then the surveyors come in here and tell us all the things we were doing wrong. This was devasting to our staff as we felt that we were doing everything that we could to protect our residents and healthcare workers."

That was a far cry from what US hospital communities were experiencing: applause and accolades. They were seen as heroes while owners, administrators, and workers in nursing homes were vilified and condemned.

Sylvia believed the nursing home industry had been this way, in a smaller degree, all along, that some of the more stringent regulations have come about because of a few badly managed facilities, and because of greed.

Many in the industry agree. But just as many believe that the vast majority of people running nursing homes include wonderful and caring administrators who are there for all the right reasons. Given what we've seen during the pandemic, has the regulatory process become a runaway train contributing to the catastrophic failure of the nursing home industry? When did the pendulum swing so far from one extreme to the other?

During my seventh visit to an Idaho nursing home in May of 2021, I saw this sort of inequity first-hand. The facility had received an IJ a few months earlier because they didn't have dedicated staff working in its COVID-19 unit. (The guidance would change only weeks later to "if possible...have dedicated staff.")

It was the Monday after Mother's Day weekend, and I had anticipated an easy day working on-site with the nursing home. I felt terrific after such a nice weekend. The Friday before, I had worked with the IP on antibiotic stewardship processes. I felt it was refreshing to get back to the "prevention" piece of infection prevention and control. My plan for that Monday was to watch infection control practices during "med passes" (the distribution of medication) and support Jessica in her IP role. Nothing too stressful.

To change things up a bit, I decided to wear a black t-shirt inscribed with the words "faith over fear" instead of scrubs. After finishing a cup of coffee, I made the seven-minute drive to the nursing home, parked my car, and retrieved my face shield from the trunk. I put on a white vest and walked toward the building.

Walking into the building, I began the COVID-19 self-screening process. This was required for anyone entering the nursing home. The administrator, Jason, was standing right at the front entrance. "Well, the dam broke," he said.

"Uh-oh," I said, "what does that mean?" I thought he was going to say that the state surveyor was in-house; they had been waiting for weeks for recertification so they could begin accepting new admissions after their IJ citation.

"A staff member tested positive," he said. "She came in today because she wasn't feeling well, and she tested positive for COVID. To make matters worse, her husband works in the kitchen, and he has a fever, although he tested negative."

It turned out the entire kitchen staff was related and had gotten together for a Mother's Day brunch the day before. They'd been sent home to quarantine, and the nursing staff was making breakfast for the residents.

Go team! I thought. This is what the nursing home staff are made of!

"We have to rapid test all the residents and staff," I told the administrator. "The PCR test would take two or three days minimum to get the results back, and we don't want to wait that long."

The positive staff member worked in a position that put her in direct contact with every resident and worker, meaning the entire facility had been exposed.

As resident testing began, I pulled Tommy, the DON, aside.

"We have to consider putting all of the residents on transmission-based precautions and isolate them in their rooms," I said.

Because the facility didn't have enough PPE, I insisted we call the county, report the positive case, and get instructions to ensure we were following the protocols accurately.

I was thinking about the state survey process. We knew the surveyors were due in any day, and this new outbreak would guarantee they would show up even sooner. We had to ensure that every IPC element was in place to protect the residents and to pass the targeted infection control survey, to be on point with everything. There was no room for errors. It was essential to get feedback from the county health department so that we could demonstrate to the state surveyors that we followed the county support and guidance.

Tommy called the county epidemiologist while I brought up the CDC's website and retrieved the most recent nursing home outbreak guidance, updated about six weeks prior.

Considering the degree of exposure, the CDC recommended placing all the residents on droplet/contact precautions for fourteen days, along with closing the building to visitors and testing all residents and staff for COVID-19 every three to seven days.

It was disappointing having to shut down the facility again; residents would not be allowed to have visitors. Only two weeks had passed since the facility had reopened, and now, in an instant, visitations were being taken away again. Just the previous week, I'd seen residents playing Wii Bowling and really enjoying themselves. Now they'd be asked to stay in their rooms with their doors closed. This was heartbreaking.

When the county epidemiologist called us back, she didn't mention the CDC guidance we expected her to, placing the entire building on precautions. Instead, she talked about how the county COVID positivity rate was at 6.6 percent, meaning there was a "mild to moderate" spread of COVID in the community.

Finally, I spoke up. "We have to follow the CDC guidance to the letter, or the state will cite us," I said. "The guidance says to place all residents on precautions if there's a known exposure."

I was again aware of how a facility could easily become confused when clear and precise guidance wasn't provided, especially from county officials. The hierarchy suggests following county guidance first, then state, then federal—whichever is strictest. Most nursing homes will contact their county health department and get recommendations at that level, but not necessarily go further. Why would they, if the hierarchy told them to follow the county guidelines first? In the middle of a crisis, they shouldn't have to make multiple phone calls to different public health agencies. In addition, during an outbreak, the facility automatically enters into emergency operations to protect the staff and residents with the least restrictive measures possible. Given how punitive the survey process was, we were no longer worried about following facility policy, which had been our historical process. It was now all about ensuring we met the guidance to pass a state survey.

I found myself in an uncomfortable situation. I was the one to direct the county health epidemiologist for the appropriate procedures. I said, "I hate to be the bad guy here, but this is what is suggested, and we have to follow it!"—to which everyone agreed.

We placed plastic PPE bins in between every resident room, stocked bins with disposable gowns, and decided to operate under the CDC's "Conventional Capacity" and not reuse any gowns. We would only reuse PPE if we couldn't get more supplies. Inability to get more supplies would then put us in "Contingent" or "Crisis" Capacity.

I began running down a checklist in my head. PPE, including gowns, gloves, N95 respirators, and face shields were now in all of the bins outside of every room, and the staff was coming in for COVID-19 testing.

I had Betsy, the receptionist, print signage on yellow paper for contact/droplet precautions, along with the CDC instructions for how to properly don and doff PPE.[1] After we printed signs and placed them in plastic sheet covers, I went around the facility and taped the signage outside of every resident room or in between two rooms—probably overkill, considering 100 percent of the residents were being placed on contact/droplet precautions, but I knew we would get in trouble with the state if we didn't have the signage posted.

One resident poked her head out of the room and asked me what I was doing.

"Posting signage for the staff to wear PPE."

"I don't have to wear it, do I?"

"No, just the staff."

"Because someone is positive?"

"Yes," I said.

"Well, it must have been a CNA if she was around everyone."

"All I can say," I said, "is that it was staff, and we are protecting you."

"Do you want any help?"

"No, I'm good," I said with a smile. "But thanks."

As I made my way down the hall, she poked her head out again and said, "Hi! Just checking on you."

"Oh, thanks," I said. "I was getting lonely."

It felt good to converse with her…to stay positive and keep the mood light. She was a relatively active lady who enjoyed interacting with residents and going to the dining hall for meals.

"I'm sorry that we have to have you all in your rooms right now," I said to her.

"Oh, that's okay. I have a lot of things to do."

She was definitely a trooper.

I went back to the conference room where the leadership was having an energetic conversation about how to preserve the PPE, with the idea that perhaps the staff could wear the gowns for resident care and contact only, such as when bathing.

"You can't do that," I said. "The state will fine you."

Even though this was the CDC's recommendation early on in the pandemic, the current request was to wear full PPE for all residents anytime *anyone* walked in the door, even just to bring a resident a glass of water (this has again since changed as of September 10, 2021).

At 2:30 p.m., I informed the team that I had to catch a plane to Utah to support another nursing home; they said they understood, but their eyes told a different story. I knew they were stressed, and having me leave now didn't help. "I am available to support you by email and phone," I reassured them. "Do not hesitate to call me for anything. Anything!" I said. After the day's events, I felt confident that they were prepared to handle the outbreak and that we had everything appropriately in place to contain the outbreak and pass the re-certification from the state.

In my journal, I made the following entry:

> May 11, 2021: Today, I felt good supporting the facility and helping them have a solid start with their outbreak, something I wish every facility in the country had. Maybe there needs to be a hotline of experts to call...the county didn't seem to be much help...

> May 12, 2021: I got a text from Jessica saying that the state surveyor was "in-house." *Of course they are,* I thought, *right in the middle of your outbreak.*

This was when the "gotcha" actions started. Nursing homes were required to report COVID-19 cases, and those reports told the surveyors where to go, and when.

Almost immediately, Jessica found one of the surveyors in a resident's room without wearing any PPE. Jessica told her that she needed to wear PPE and the surveyor responded with, "How am I supposed to know? Nobody told me."

"There are signs everywhere," Jessica said.

The surveyor responded with, "There was no sign that indicated the resident was on isolation."

When Jessica relayed that information to me, I felt angry. Betsy and I had meticulously printed and posted signage outside or in between every resident's room.

The surveyor also pointed out to Jessica that the door of the resident's room was not closed. Thankfully, I had warned Jessica that surveyors look for that situation, so they had to at least try to close the doors. If the resident didn't tolerate a closed door, then this information had to be documented in the patient's care plan (more about this in a future chapter).

The reason for closing the door was to prevent the possible spread of COVID through the air when a resident was indeed infected. Keeping the door closed created a "barrier" between an infected individual and the rest of the facility. However, with this vulnerable population, keeping doors closed gave the staff no way to check on the resident. Closed doors can create unintended consequences when staff is unable to monitor resident safety.

A flood of emotions came over me, including anger, knowing all of the work that we had done in advance of the survey. I had observed a full team effort to keep everybody safe while staying true to the protocols and guidance. The surveyors walked in at a time when the facility was short-staffed and at the highest level of stress. Their good work was being nitpicked.

I felt like I'd been kicked in the shins. The entire scenario was a vulnerable situation with low PPE resources and residents confined behind closed doors. Having people come in and point out imperfections felt like a bonus punch to the gut.

Thinking back to my days of working in an ICU during the H1N1 pandemic, I remembered how we, the staff, were doing everything we could to keep patients alive. I can't even imagine what that would have felt like if state surveyors had walked in to point out areas they felt were not perfect, such as an improperly tied gown or complaining that a nurse pulled a gown over her head because it was too hard to tie with her hands behind her back. It would definitely be more productive to have had support coming in to say, "Hey, you are in a crisis; how can we help?"

My question is this: Since when was the nursing home industry required to operate at 100 percent perfection? Show me any healthcare institution, any business for the matter, that operates without a single mistake.

If it seems that I am overemphasizing the punitive environment that was happening in nursing homes during the pandemic, I am doing it for a good reason.

The following timeline describes my ongoing dialogue with the nursing home's administrator and staff on June 13, 2021, during what would be the first of three days of an on-site recertification process. This is not a standardized process after a facility has received a 2567 citation. Some surveyors take three hours, some three days.

- 10:26 a.m.: I got an urgent email from Tommy, the nursing home's DON. The subject line read: "survey help asap," and the body of the text read: "Morning Buffy! Surveyors are asking for CDC signage for special droplet precautions! I think Jessica is about to call you!"

- 10:38 a.m.: I responded by text: "What's wrong with the signage? The CDC does not have special contact/droplet precautions. Here is the CDC PPE signage."

- 10:44 a.m.: Knowing good and well that the CDC did not develop this special "contact/droplet" signage, I thought I would verify directly with the CDC. I emailed both Kara Slifka-Jacobson, M.D., and Angela Anttila, Ph.D., MSN, NP-C, CIC at the CDC: "Hi Kara, I hope that you are doing well. I am curious if the CDC has a Special Contact/Droplet Precautions signage. State surveyors are getting *super* picky and requesting that the signage come from the CDC. This is all that I could find. *https://www.cdc.gov/infectioncontrol/basics/transmission-based-precautions.html-anchor_1564058318*. Typically, facilities have been using signage from the Washington Hospital Association or other advocate groups. Please let me know if you do have this special signage. If not, no worries at all. I will simply inform the state health department."

- 10:49 a.m.: I got a call from Jason relaying the same message that Tommy sent: "The state surveyors are asking if we have Special Droplet Precautions signage from the CDC. They don't like the signage we are using as it is not from the CDC."

- 11:24 a.m.: Dr. Jacobs-Slifka responded: "Hi Buffy! I hope you are doing well! I don't think we, at CDC, feel strongly about where the signs come from as long as there are signs! We have not created something like this, as far as I am aware. Facilities could post both Contact and Droplet or could create their own signage—the important thing being that it clearly communicates what anyone entering needs to do (PPE). "It is also possible that the Healthcare-Associated Infections (HAI) program or EPI (Expanded Program on Immunization) side of the health department might have created something. Best, Kara."

I immediately forwarded this email to Tommy, Jason, and Jessica, then texted it to them, knowing it would reach them faster on their phones.

- 12:20 p.m.: I received a text from Jessica: "The state asked why you recommended the isolation for all residents and if there was something in the CDC or CMS guidelines stating that we needed to do this."

At this point, I felt confused. Was the surveyor legitimately concerned about my recommendation, or was she simply trying to trick the facility? You can absolutely be sure that if we had not placed all the residents in isolation after a facility-wide exposure, they would have given the facility an IJ citation!

- 12:27 p.m.: I sent Jessica the following information, which I had also sent on Monday before putting the entire building on precautions so that the leadership knew where my guidance was coming from: "Recommended precautions should be continued for residents until no new cases of SARS-CoV-2 infection have been identified for at least fourteen days. The incubation period for SARS-CoV-2 infection can be up to fourteen days, and the identification of a new case within that period after starting the interventions does not necessarily represent a failure of the interventions implemented to control transmission."[2] Her immediate response was: "Got it; thank you so much for your assistance."

- 1:17 p.m.: I got an email from Tommy: "Thanks for all your help this morning, Buffy. They are now asking for the manufacturer's instructions for donning and doffing the blue plastic gowns. Jason found a card with pictures but no instructions. Any ideas? Tommy." After reading that text, I had an outburst and said, "Now, this is beyond ridiculous!"

- 1:20 p.m.: I responded to Tommy with the following: "This is *insane*! Donning and doffing instructions come from the CDC regardless of type. The manufacturer is probably from China, and it is unlikely that they provide IFU's [Instructions For Use]."

- 1:21 p.m.: Tommy's response made me laugh out loud: "Welcome to Idaho."

I mean, seriously, this was insane. I was feeling defeated because the surveyors were tearing them apart for not having CDC signage that didn't exist, questioning why they had the entire building on precautions, and now asking for something that wasn't even available. It was absolute nonsense. There was or is no federal rule that states a facility of any type *must* use the CDC infographics or signage for PPE. Nothing states the PPE *must* come with manufacturer's instructions for use, especially PPE from China. We follow procedures based on evidence-based guidance—for example, we had signs posted for how to don and doff PPE, which was more than sufficient.

My attention was diverted all day with such nonsense coming in from Idaho. The staff on-site was jumping through hoops, taking valuable time away from supporting the staff and residents during an outbreak. What part of this makes any sense or is appropriate? None of it!

After three long days of tormenting the Idaho site's staff, the facility was labeled "non-compliant" after a long list of infractions were discovered and threatened with being "terminated" from Medicare and Medicaid reimbursement in one month's time if they didn't make changes.

I was furious, and wondered why the state waited to come on-site after the facility declared they were in substantial compliance over two months ago? Why wait to evaluate the facility's procedures until they were in the middle of a facility-wide outbreak?

The following week, I returned to the Idaho nursing home to find that the attitude of the staff had shifted. Everyone was worn out. Morale was low. Jason told me having the surveyors on-site felt like a "witch hunt." He said at one point two surveyors were standing only a few feet away from a CNA who was donning PPE and preparing to go into a resident's room. They stood with their clipboards and pens in hand, poised and ready to find something wrong with her process of putting on her PPE.

"I wish you'd been here," Jason said, "to witness the ludicrousness. They were standing there, ready to pounce."

It's hard enough to know what to do in these uncertain times without a surveyor coming in trying to trip you up. Even the county epidemiologist wasn't entirely sure what measures to implement.

I needed answers, so I called Diane Eckles, the current Arizona Bureau Chief, to talk about the survey process.

"When COVID hit," Diane explained, "I don't think we were ever expecting the level of infection control found in hospitals would be needed in skilled nursing homes. Facilities had been ramping up the federal infection control rules; however, there were many protocols that hadn't been fully implemented, such as the requirement to have an infection preventionist on-site at least part-time."

It was well known that some nursing homes were more advanced than others with the new IPC federal requirements, and others were falling behind. Still, the surveyors, prior to COVID-19, were not instructed to cite a facility, according to CMS, for a federal infection control rule that was not being fully implemented.

"Perhaps that was a missed opportunity because of the delays in getting the regulations done, and maybe facilities kind of put it [infection control] on the back burner," Diane admitted.

When she first heard of COVID-19, Diane remembers thinking, *Oh, I hope this isn't the pandemic we've been training for all these years.* She found the virus aspect interesting, given her background in microbiology.

"I had no idea it would wallop us like it did," she said.

When that wallop came in March of 2020, on a Monday morning Diane called her survey teams in Tucson and Phoenix and told them to get out of the nursing homes, halt all routine state surveys, and that it might be a while before they would conduct surveys again. She knew this was a serious situation, but didn't know that in a matter of weeks, Arizona would have its first nursing home COVID outbreak, and that her division would be asked to go on-site at a facility.

"We had to go to the state lab and borrow some PPE," she remembered. "We had no gowns, gloves, or masks."

A Tucson nursing home with several cases was Diane and company's first stop. "It was very unsettling for all of us," she admitted. "We didn't know if we would be bringing COVID back to our office or if we would catch it."

She and her staff remained gloved, gowned, and masked during what was the state's first nursing home COVID-19 regulatory survey.

"In the beginning, we tried to be more educational," she told me. "We called every facility in April and May 2020, before we could get PPE, and walked through the CDC's COVID-19 infection control risk assessment with the facility, giving hints on what to do."

At that stage of the pandemic, licensing was only required to go onsite if there was an outbreak or if the county was concerned about a facility. Soon enough, CMS announced that every facility required a visit by July 1. Diane said some of her staff were hesitant. None of her surveyors brought COVID-19 into a nursing home; however, this was at a time when the facilities were closed to visitors unless they were an "essential worker." Surveyors were allowed to enter the facility, and the nursing home was not allowed to ask them if they had a negative COVID-19 test to demonstrate that they were not putting the facility at risk. If they did, they had the right to refuse to answer, and were still allowed entrance into the facility.

Licensing continued working closely with their county partners, but Diane said it was well understood in the industry that the county health department was the "good guys" and that licensing was the "bad guys." The county was there to help, while licensing was there to point out the problems and issue citations.

Diane explained that her division didn't know enough COVID-19 protocols to offer help to the facilities and were careful not to be intrusive in the middle of a pandemic.

"I think CMS could have been more helpful instead of regulatory," Diane admitted to me. "All these directed plans of correction. I don't think COVID-19 cares if there is a plan of correction or not. It does its own thing, no matter how good a facility or how bad a facility is. It's gonna get in there."

I wanted to thank Diane for her honesty, for admitting that she, the Bureau Chief, felt the bullying and the lousy timing were unfair.

She said one of the earliest pandemic challenges was that the county would come out with guidance, and then the state HAI group or the EPIs would come up with something else, and both would differ from the CDC and CMS guidelines.

"The challenge became 'How do we now get everyone on the same page as quickly as possible?' I was frustrated with that," Diane said. "We kind of looked at whatever guidance was stricter and went with that."

It's simply jaw-dropping that this was the operational expectation for our nursing homes. The facilities didn't have the resources or the staff to properly handle this situation, and the guidance was constantly changing.

I found that to be the case with many states. Facilities had a hard time keeping track of all the changes. If a surveyor came in and thought the nursing home was following the proper guidance as stated in their policy, they could still get a citation if it wasn't the strictest guidance currently available. Sylvia had mentioned that the surveyors were going into this situation as blind as everyone else, that they couldn't be confident of the exact practices that needed to be implemented either.

"At first, it was a challenge," Diane agreed. "CMS gave us a checklist and not much more. I think we had really good communication. The surveyors would see something and call a team lead here or one of our managers, and then we'd all get together and talk about what they were seeing and what we felt the rule was supposed to be."

I didn't know how feeling like the "bad" guy in this crisis could feel good to anyone, yet Diane said she was able to sleep at night because she'd received a letter from CMS saying her division's F880 tags were significantly lower compared to the rest of the country. Arizona was way below the average, given the amount of money they were spending in a facility for infection control compared to the rest of the nation.

CMS then required Diane's division to provide the state licensing office a plan of correction. The tables were turned; now they were being asked to do the very thing they were asking nursing homes to do.

Sylvia had already described this scenario to me, from her perspective: the more tags you hand out, the better you appear at your job. Lower citation numbers meant poor performance of surveyors, not high performance of facilities.

Diane agreed the government response could have been different. "I think they could have been much more supportive instead of just throwing down a gauntlet," she said. "We're seeing the fines now, and it's kind of ridiculous."

I asked what would happen if CMS didn't respond to nursing homes with fines and citations. Would this have gone differently, and would that have made a difference?

"That's a good question," Diane replied. "The information was coming fast and furious, and it was hard to keep up. I think CMS should have given them more time to get things in place and get training done. The first outbreak in the nursing home in Washington kind of set the tone for the rest of the country. It was bad for the regulators, bad for the SNFs, and it was bad all around. We had no idea that this virus would hit the elderly like it has."

CHAPTER 10

DELIVERY OF CARE IN COMMUNITY LIVING ENVIRONMENTS

"We have to learn from this pandemic...we can't simply pack it away as a terrible time and just go back to the way we were before."
—Kesia Scales, PHI National

The resident was crying in pain. The staff was calming him down.

"I know, buddy. Sorry you don't feel good. We're going to get you all cleaned up, my friend."

These are the words that I overheard one morning while working on-site in a nursing home. Caring is the only way anyone can survive working in this environment.

What image comes to mind when you think about a nursing home? Most people picture senior citizens lined up in wheelchairs along a lonely hallway. While this is partly accurate, the care delivered in nursing homes has drastically changed over the last decade.

The reality is, any one of us could be admitted to a nursing home, or skilled nursing facility, if we need medical care beyond what hospitals offer. The fact is that nursing homes are not hospitals, although they often function as "mini-hospitals" for sick patients and those who need rehabilitation services.

In March of 2020, my daughter Chelsey texted that one of her close friends had been in a severe car accident and was going into a nursing home for rehabilitation. Lacy was twenty-four years old at the time; I remember thinking, *God help her*, as this was the exact time that resident visitations had halted and the PPE shortage began.

I've known Lacy for more than fifteen years. She used to come to our house often and hang out with Chelsey. She was quiet and shy but always sweet and warm.

I knew Lacy's nursing home stay during COVID-19 would offer a unique perspective that warranted attention, so she and I met via Zoom to discuss her extraordinary experience. She explained that she'd been riding her moped when she was struck by a car that blew through an intersection. She broke her rotator cuff, two places in her back, her tailbone and foot, and snapped her right knee in half. She couldn't move her arm, was wearing a back brace, a splint, and a leg immobilizer—all rendering her completely bedbound.

Lacy had spent two weeks in the hospital in intensive rehabilitation therapy before it was recommended that she complete her recovery in a nursing home that specialized in physical therapy. She would have preferred simply going home, but because of the extent of her injuries, she spent six weeks in a nursing home.

She was the youngest person in the facility; however, some residents in their late thirties and forties were also there on short-term stays for various rehabilitation needs. The first two weeks of Lacy's admission were spent in quarantine in a unit with all the other new admissions.

It was an uncomfortable experience for her in the nursing home. "It was terrible. I hated being there," she told me. Unable to have visitors, she filled her time with books and television. Having a schedule with the therapists and mealtimes gave her something to look forward to. Daily activities within a nursing home are essential to keeping the residents mentally, physically, and psychologically engaged. "My cousin pulled some money together and bought me a Nintendo Switch and some games so I could play while I was there. My friend left me her iPad with her Hulu account, so I was watching more TV shows. That was basically what I did. I played some games, I watched some shows, and I read books, and I spent a lot of time talking to my sister and friends."

Eliminating visitors was a necessary step, no doubt, but it had its drawbacks. In January 2021, a report titled *The Devastating Effect of Lockdowns on Residents of Long-Term Care Facilities During COVID-19*, the National Consumer Voice for Quality Long-term Care described how families across the country complained that "residents were unkempt, clearly hadn't been bathed or groomed in months, had lost significant weight, and were significantly depressed, even suicidal."[1]

The report included the experiences of 191 families; 85 percent noted a decline in physical abilities, while 87 percent indicated their loved one's physical appearance had worsened. Ninety-one percent reported that their loved one's mental status had declined; 40 percent noted their loved ones were missing personal belongings, and 69 percent felt the facility didn't appear to have sufficient staff to care for the residents.

Given these alarming percentages, it's easy to see why nursing homes were accused of providing subpar and inadequate care. No doubt that vast improvements are needed across this industry. Some facilities need more help than others, but we need to address the "why" behind this inadequate care and start investing in the workforce to improve care rather than simply rely on a broken and ineffective regulatory system.

One of Lacy's greatest challenges and concerns was with the certified nursing assistants (CNAs). "There was one of them that I really didn't like dealing with. The first night I was there, I was wearing some shorts that I had worn at the hospital because it was hard for me to wear pants with all the attached equipment. At the hospital, this wasn't a problem—me wearing shorts. The CNAs were fine with helping me take off the shorts, and it wasn't a big deal moving them around my equipment. The first time that I had help changing at the nursing facility, the CNA who was helping me was really rough, she was not gentle, and I had my legs in an immobilizer and it hurt."

Lacy paused and began to cry. She apologized for the tears. She wiped her eyes with a tissue and took a deep breath to continue.

"It's okay; take your time," I said.

"She [the CNA] was being really rough, kind of dropping my leg like an inch or two, which was painful, and she was struggling with helping to take off the shorts, and she said, 'You better start wearing a gown or something. If we have to take these shorts off like this all the time, we're going to end up breaking your leg again.' And for me, um...being in that position of helplessness, it was just very staggering to hear someone say that to me."

My heart ached for what Lacy went through, and I was grateful for her courage to speak about it. Knowing the demands of the healthcare staff, I asked her if she felt that the employees had the time to devote to her, to provide the slow and gentle care that she needed.

"That was something I thought about a lot because there were other people in the hall that I was in. There was this woman who would scream all night. At some point, she was moved out, and then another person came in who would literally throw themselves off their bed. The CNAs were dealing with a lot of stuff, and I think it was very tiring."

Lacy continued her story, "One of the things I thought about was they [CNAs] had a very slow response time. I would need help going to the bathroom, and sometimes I would hit the call button, and it would be two hours before anyone came in. I'm, like, holding my bladder, waiting for someone to come. I was thinking about why they thought that was okay. One of the things I thought about, specifically in the rehab section of the nursing home, is that not everybody needed as much care as I did, but people would be hitting the call button for very small things. So, I think it was just hard for them to keep up with everything. Somebody might be hitting the call button every thirty minutes because they want their water replaced. So, I thought maybe they might not take it seriously if I hit my call button because not everything is important enough for them to come right away.

"There was one CNA that I really liked. She was generally good with the call times, yet she seemed stressed all the time. She was always very sweet, and it really seemed like she was trying her best, but I could just tell she was, like, haggard," Lacy explained,

Lacy also shared that it was obvious that the CNAs appeared severely understaffed and overworked. This perception is accurate and a perpetual industry discussion.

Within long-term care, facilities have always had trouble retaining staff. Medicaid reimbursements barely cover the cost of providing care, which makes paying staff a decent wage problematic.[2]

The article "Appropriate Nurse Staffing Levels for US Nursing Homes" describes how the more staff there is, the better care the residents receive.[3]

But currently, long-term care staffing requirements are ambiguous and subjective; federal regulation states that a nursing home must have "sufficient" staff to meet the needs of the residents but fails to define what "sufficient" means. This has been the federal regulation per CMS for more than thirty years. Clearly, the nursing home industry and the level of resident care have significantly changed. Although each state has different laws defining the number of per-day staff hours for resident care, from 2017–2018 it was found that 75 percent of all nursing homes never met the CMS requirement for RN staffing.[4]

In a brief report titled "Staffing Levels and COVID-19 Cases and Outbreaks in U.S. Nursing Homes," Dr. Konetzka and Rebecca Gorges described chronic understaffing as a situation that had occurred for decades. "We know that having adequate staffing is fundamental to delivering high-quality care to the residents," Dr. Konetzka tells me, then goes on to explain that the strongest indicator for a COVID-19 infection entering the nursing home was how high the COVID-19 rates were in the nursing home's county. However, with more staff, the research demonstrated that fewer deaths occurred.[5] What does this mean? We couldn't necessarily prevent COVID from coming into the nursing homes, but with adequate staffing, we could have prevented more deaths.

When Lacy was in the acute care rehabilitation hospital, she saw more CNAs working than in the nursing home. She truly believed that if the nursing home CNAs had more support, including more staff, they could have performed their job duties better. If this had been possible, it would have produced a positive cascade effect. Instead of residents getting frustrated with CNAs taking two hours to answer a call light, additional support would ensure a faster response and less stressful residency. Likewise, CNAs who aren't continually subjected to negative feedback from residents might also stay at their jobs longer.

The Coalition of Geriatric Nursing Organizations and the American Nursing Association both recommend that each resident receive 4.1 hours of nursing care a day, and that at least 30 percent of the staff be licensed nurses.[6] Current legislation has been introduced to increase staffing needs from "sufficient" to more targeted ratios, such as the four-to-one ratio. In addition, The Consumer Voice Group has been advocating for at least one around-the-clock RN rather than the current requirement of eight hours a day, seven days a week.[7] We, the consumers of this care, have to ask ourselves what happens during the other sixteen hours when there isn't an RN on staff.

One reason for CNA understaffing is the lousy pay. In a 2016 report titled, *Raise the Floor: Quality Nursing Home Care Depends on Quality Jobs*, Paraprofessional Healthcare Institute describes how higher-quality jobs lead to higher levels of care for residents:

The estimated 650,000 CNAs nationwide do our heavy lifting and carrying, provide intimate bodily care, and possibly the most important, provide emotional support. These workers wake residents in the morning and put them to bed at night; ensure residents are bathed, groomed, and dressed; lift them from their beds; and take them to meals, activities, and various therapy and medical appointments.[8]

Clearly essential to the quality of care delivered, nursing homes couldn't operate without CNAs. Yet they are often underpaid and are typically offered part-time schedules with no benefits like paid time off, sick leave, educational opportunities, or health insurance. The median annual earnings for CNAs is estimated to be $19,000 with a median wage of $11.51 per hour, and less than 45 percent of them have full-time, year-round work. To make ends meet, about 38 percent of CNAs rely on public assistance, including Medicaid, food stamps, and cash assistance to provide additional support for their households.[9]

Kezia Scales, Director of Policy Research, and Stephen Campbell work for PHI National (PHI), a New York-based nonprofit that aims to promote nursing home workforce change through innovation, improved policy, and research. The two have echoed a call for higher wages and improved working conditions.

Scales described the turnover problem "has been exacerbated during the pandemic with CNAs getting sick or having to stay home to care for children, school-aged kids, or family members that they didn't want to risk transmitting the infection to. When this critical workforce is then reduced, who steps in to take their place in one of the worst possible environments during the pandemic?"

She goes on to speculate what it was like for CNAs already stretched thin, possibly working with less training, trying to don and doff their PPE every time they saw a new resident. Infection prevention and control was such a challenge prior to the pandemic, then add all of these layers on top of that. Really bringing it to a breaking point, which is why we saw the conditions we have."

Dr. Patricia Stone remembered her first job as a nurse's aide at age fifteen. "Perhaps the hardest of all is how poorly they're treated," Stone said. "They don't have a real career ladder and are not often highly respected. The work is hard and can be abusive, both physically and emotionally."

Lacy agreed. "I tried to be patient with them [CNAs] because I didn't think it would do any good for me to be upset. But there were residents who would cuss the staff out. I think out of all the CNAs I met there, there was only one who never really seemed phased by anything. I think he may have been an immigrant because he had an accent, but I'm not sure where he was from. He worked the night shifts, which are generally a bit easier going, and he was the only CNA who actually answered the call light pretty quickly, like, within twenty minutes. And he would come in and be, like, 'Alright my love, what do you need?' He was just so sweet all the time. There were a lot of CNAs that I did like that had a friendly and outgoing attitude; they just seemed really stressed out and tired."

The *Washington Post* article "In a Relentless Pandemic, Nursing-home Workers Are Worn Down and Stressed Out" discusses stories of employees leaving their positions out of anger and fear of their workplace environment.[10] It describes that a survey of 30 percent of nurses working in nursing homes met the definition of burnout.

"I did feel like they were very overworked," Lacy added. "One of the impressions I got from a couple of them that were hard to deal with or unsympathetic was that it felt more like the characteristics of burnout, like, professional burnout; you're so burned out that you don't care. And that's really hard when you're relying on somebody that doesn't care anymore because they're so overworked. I think that's one of the best ways to describe it."

I personally experienced this firsthand during a recent on-site nursing home visit, where I noticed a CNA not wearing the appropriate PPE. When I questioned her about why she wasn't wearing a gown into an isolated resident's room, she replied, "I'm sorry, I'm very busy and need to deliver these meal trays."

When I got some time to talk to her one-on-one, she was frank: She hated both her job and her profession and wanted out. She was in the last semester of her bachelor's in nursing degree and couldn't take the industry anymore. She planned to quit and complete her degree in healthcare administration instead.

"I just want out," she told me. "I don't qualify to work anywhere else right now, so I stay here. I've even applied for construction jobs."

I was sad to hear this from a formerly ambitious and dedicated healthcare worker.

"I wanted to get my RN degree and then go to medical school and become a surgeon," she said. "I've been dreaming of this my entire life. COVID changed all that."

This book contains several calls to action, but here is the main one:

We, as a society, must invest in the staff who care for the vulnerable residents of nursing and rehabilitation homes. This investment should come from the payers, Medicare and Medicaid, with transparency in the way our federal dollars are spent; because the truth is, we don't know how much is going to direct care, administrative costs, or shareholders pockets.

The National Consumer Voice for Quality Long-Term Care agrees and is advocating for a dedicated percentage to go toward direct care, which is the highest cost in nursing homes.

The way I see it, everything should play out like this: to provide the safest environment for our residents, we need to provide the best environment for the staff. To do so, we need to increase pay and benefits so the staff is not severely overworked. To do this, we need law reform that looks at not only the costs of what reimbursement covers, but to change the way the industry must spend these reimbursements. We need to eliminate any self-dealing that may occur, establish cost category reimbursement methods that require facilities to spend on specific things like staff and residents, and enact direct-care ratios, allowing specific portions of reimbursement to go directly toward the well-being of residents.

The bottom line is that if the staff are happy and able to do their job effectively, they can provide the best level of care to our residents. When we offer anything less than this, everything begins to fall apart. Fast.

* * *

One year after her accident, Lacy continues to work with a therapist to overcome the trauma—not only of the accident and her injuries, but of her nursing home experience. She now has full range of motion in her arm and has less pain in her back, allowing her to sit for longer periods of time. Her leg is still a work in progress. She has a cane for walking, but at age twenty-five, she doesn't exactly feel comfortable using it to get around.

Instead, she walks unassisted with a limp. Remarkably, Lacey has returned to her martial arts training, working to get her black belt.

Lacy's memory of the nursing home lingers. She mostly remembers wanting to get out of there so badly and couldn't imagine what it would feel like to have to live there permanently. Those six weeks in a nursing home left her life forever altered.

CHAPTER 11

SHIFTING FROM REACTIVE TO PROACTIVE INFECTION PREVENTION AND CONTROL

"Be proactive, not reactive, for an apparently insignificant issue ignored today can spawn tomorrow's catastrophe."
—Ken Poirot

As I've described, infections are the leading cause of morbidity and mortality among the millions of residents in US nursing homes. Between 1.6 and 3.8 million infections occur every year, with an estimated 380,000 deaths attributed to them. Healthcare costs associated with infection in nursing homes range from $673 million to $2 billion.[1]

It wasn't that long ago that acquiring an infection was an accepted risk of a hospital visit. That began to shift in the early seventies, when infection control emerged as a distinct specialty. A few hospital infection control nurses recognized the need for a more organized approach to reducing healthcare-associated infections (HAIs) and founded the Association for Professionals in Infection Control and Epidemiology (APIC), a non-profit organization that now has more than fifteen thousand members in forty-eight countries. Their mission is to create a safer world by preventing infections.[2]

The 1999 Institute of Medicine report titled *To Err is Human*[3] challenged healthcare providers to consider the "institutional, financial, and human costs associated with preventable mistakes."[4] The long-time assumption that infections were unavoidable was challenged, and a new perception that HAIs could be preventable was born; from this assertion came the phrase "infection prevention."

In 2002, seven US states began to require hospitals to publicly report their HAIs, which at that time accounted for 1.7 million annual infections and nearly one hundred thousand deaths.[5] Three years later in 2005, the CDC established the National Healthcare Safety Network (NHSN) by merging three historical HAI surveillance systems, the National Nosocomial Infections Surveillance (NNIS) system, the Dialysis Surveillance Network (DSN), and the National Surveillance System for Healthcare Workers (NaSH). NHSN is now considered the nation's most widely used HAI tracking system to measure the progress of healthcare infection prevention efforts.[6]

Beginning in 2008, hospital regulatory and accrediting agencies like CMS began to require hospitals to report certain HAI's, including Catheter-Associated Urinary Tract Infection (CAUTI) and Central-Line Associated Bloodstream Infections (CLABSI).[7] This reported data was incorporated into the hospital's Medicare payment and reimbursement model. It incentivized hospitals to implement infection prevention protocols such as handwashing, safe injection practices, and device-associated safety measures, to mitigate the risk of a patient acquiring, becoming harmed by, and potentially dying from an infection obtained during their hospital stay.

In 2009, the American Recovery and Reinvestment Act (ARRA) provided $50 million to the fifty states, the District of Columbia, and Puerto Rico to support the implementation of this proactive approach to reducing HAIs. This funding was used for developing, expanding, and supporting the infrastructure to the hospitals' HAI programs.[8] A short time later, the CMS Quality Improvement Organizations (QIOs) were commissioned to assist with this process by offering the hospitals technical support.[9]

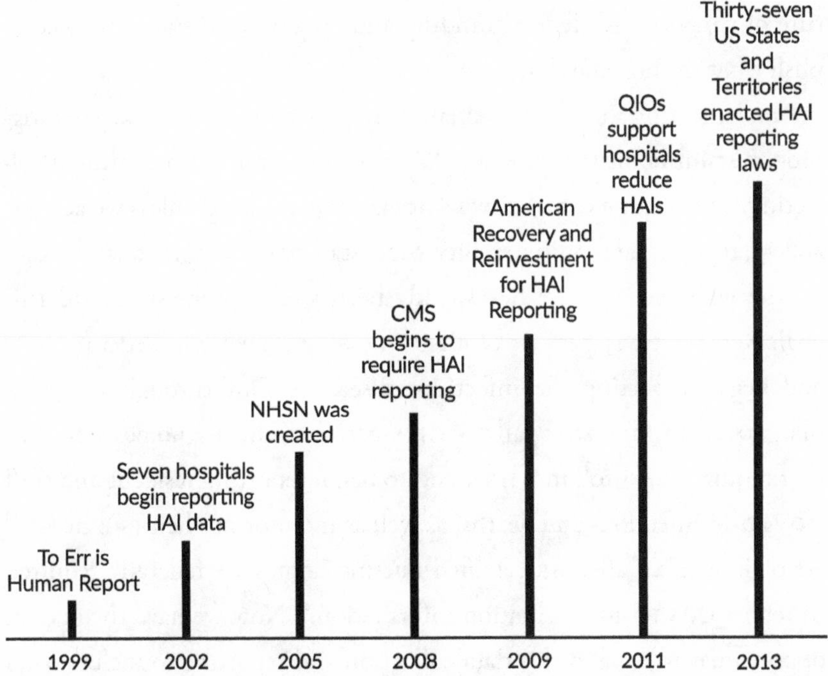

Figure 1: Hospital HAI Data Reporting Inception

By 2013, thirty-seven US states and territories enacted laws that required hospitals to report HAI data to the CDC and CMS, the majority of which had begun in 2008.[10]

As the result of hospitals reporting HAIs, the CDC now produces an annual HAI state progress report that describes HAIs statistics and if they are increasing or decreasing. The 2019 National and State Healthcare-Associated Infections Progress Report describes the results of hospital infection prevention efforts for 2019, using 2015 as a baseline.[11] For example, 100 percent of all US states performed better on at least two infection types.[12]

This type of national and state HAI progress report is not available for nursing homes. Why? Because nursing homes nationally are not federally required to report HAIs into NHSN. Nursing homes need a similar structure of support with federal funding and technical assistance to accomplish what the hospitals have.

Implementing a robust surveillance and reporting system is key to a vigorous nursing home IPC program. We can't prevent infections without collecting data, and we can't know what we are preventing unless we actively collect, report, and monitor facility-wide, state-wide, and national data.

The good news: there has already been steady progress toward this goal. Remember, 15 percent of all US nursing homes enrolled in NHSN and began reporting the infectious disease C-Diff through the CMS pilot study. In June 2020, all US CMS-certified nursing homes were further required to enroll in NHSN and to begin reporting resident and staff COVID-19 infections and deaths, as well as monitoring their PPE needs.[13] As of June 2021, all CMS-certified nursing homes are federally required to report COVID-19 vaccination information.[14] Now we have the perfect opportunity to expand this data collection and reporting to include HAI data and process measures.

Some states have already mandated that nursing homes report HAIs. Wisconsin nursing homes were required to input carbapenem-resistant Enterobacterales (CRE) data into NHSN beginning in 2011.[15] Carbapenem-resistant Enterobacterales are bacteria commonly found in the human gut that may include Escherichia, Klebsiella, Enterobacter, Salmonellosis, Shigella, Citrobacter, and Yersinia.[16] These species are usually harmless and necessary for digestion; however, these bacteria can cause infections in the bloodstream, urinary tract, or wounds and contribute to pneumonia and meningitis. Some types of enterobacteria, including *Klebsiella pneumoniae* and *Escherichia coli* (*E. coli*), can become resistant to antibiotics—the last line of defense to treat them.[17] CRE infections are most common in hospital and nursing home patients, especially those that require devices for care like breathing machines (ventilators), urinary catheters (into the bladder), or intravenous catheters (into a vein). These patients take long courses of specific antibiotics and may have a weakened immune system; however, CREs are also becoming more prominent in communities.

My colleague Gwen Borlaug—an infection preventionist and a champion of HAI data surveillance and reporting in nursing homes—was working for the Wisconsin Department of Health when the state decided, in 2013, to mandate the reporting of CRE to NHSN. The measure was meant to decrease the spread of these often-deadly infectious agents. Once it was mandatory, the state health department worked with nursing homes and helped them collect the data and report it. This collaborative approach strengthened the nursing homes' IPC program as they met every month to collaborate with the licensing division. They had the support they needed in an environment that was non-punitive. The partnership also helped the public health and licensing division learn about the challenges in the nursing homes so that they could implement the appropriate measures to support their needs.

Nursing homes continue to report CRE. The evolving process has now been made easier using the state's electronic surveillance system to automatically upload this information from testing laboratories. Capturing this data enables public health to implement proactive measures, education, and awareness to prevent ongoing diseases from spreading within a community.

The joint public health and licensing support was critically important to the success of the CRE initiative. It's not enough to simply mandate our nursing homes to report HAI measures without the appropriate infrastructure, funding, and shoulder-to-shoulder support to ensure the nursing homes are set up for success. HAI data collection and reporting must also include a qualified designated infection preventionist.

Historically, the IP has predominantly held a clinical role, such as a licensed nurse. When we first started infection control in nursing homes, being in charge of the infection control program came with being a supervisor, usually a nurse," Dr. Patricia Stone explained, "with no more training in infection prevention than any other nurse. Which is not a lot. It's basic hand hygiene, standard precautions, disinfecting and room cleaning."

Over the last few years, the IP role has expanded to include complex data surveillance and analytics, and the industry has slowly included other professionals, such as epidemiologists, public health professionals, medical technologists, microbiologists, and doctors.[18] Being a licensed nurse isn't always the norm.

The Department of Health and Human Services Centers for Medicare and Medicaid Services published a ruling in 2019 that requires all US nursing homes to "designate one or more individual(s) as infection preventionists who are responsible for the facility's infection and control program. The IP must (1) have primary professional training in nursing, medical technology, microbiology, epidemiology, or other related field; (2) be qualified by education, training, experience, or certification; (3) work at least part-time at the facility; and (4) have completed specialized training in infection prevention and control. The IP must also be a member of the facility's quality assessment and assurance committee."[19]

Later, with a heavy push from nursing home lobbyists and some advocacy groups, a proposed rule was put forth to CMS to change the "part-time" designation to "sufficient time." Of course, "sufficient time" could support more than part-time, but as we have seen with our nursing staff, it usually results in fewer staffing hours, not more.

Sylvia said when she started consulting for nursing homes in 1994, the IPC nurses were also the assistant director of nurses (ADON). "They had a very little amount of time carved out to work on infection control, which basically consisted of taking phone orders from physicians and looking for antibiotics. They looked at where the infections were and usually made colored dots on a map of the facility and focused on whether there was a cluster of infections, which would then prompt training with the staff," Sylvia said. "For example, if there were a lot of urinary tract infections, the IP would educate that staff on infection control practices to reduce them, such as ensuring the resident was hydrated, and the staff was conducting good hand hygiene practices. The infections were reported at the monthly quality meeting and then left at that."

In my experience, before COVID-19, not much had changed in the past decade. Many of the IPs also hold the position of the Director of Nursing (DON) or ADON; both are full-time jobs without adding IPC responsibilities. When I speak to the designated infection preventionist, the majority tell me that even though they have a part-time designation, they rarely spend more than five to six hours per week on infection prevention. In fact, if the facility is short on nurses, the IP is often the first to get called to work as a floor nurse. One IP recently told me she was the IP on paper only, as she had to work the floor because of the nursing shortage.

Some states, such as California, have mandated that the IP work full-time and are leading the way for this specialized role.[20] It will be a travesty if, as an industry, we don't realize the breadth and scope of what is required of the IP and invest in full-time skilled and qualified personnel.

Sarah, the nursing home IP I'd worked with in the field, explained that the available IP training is simply not sufficient for a nursing home IP to be successful. There are a few IP training programs for long-term care, but there's a lack of mentoring and one-on-one support for our nursing home IPs. They complete the training, and then what? Online and in-person training is effective, but how much of the information is retained?

Sarah described how she felt after taking one of the remote learning programs.

"I was like, I don't know what I am supposed to do. I remember looking at the McGeer surveillance criteria for antibiotic stewardship and saying, 'Now, what the heck am I supposed to do with this?' It would be much better, prior to COVID-19, to have had an actual program with more hands-on support."

This is the type of support my consulting firm, as well as Doctors Without Borders, have provided. Sarah said she learned more in one day than in one year from our on-site visit, which included a comprehensive IPC assessment and targeted IPC resources.

"I had no idea Environmental Services was a part of infection control," Sarah admitted. "I didn't know what I didn't know."

Sarah is not alone. Over the years, I've talked to literally hundreds of nurses assigned to the IP role who felt their training had been inadequate for the required responsibilities. In addition to the specialized training that nursing home IPs take, we need to create a specialized infection control certification based on this unique setting, one that will support ongoing education and training.

The Certification Board of Infection Control and Epidemiology, Inc., has a specialized Certification in Prevention and Control (CIC) for IPs that's nonspecific to the healthcare setting as it primarily focuses on acute care hospitals. Research has demonstrated the value of certification as CIC IPs are more likely to implement infection control measures, act as champions for key infection prevention practices, and are better able to interpret evidence.[21] What's more, CIC certification is highly valued as the requirements to obtain certification are rigorous. Prerequisites to sit for the arduous 150-question proctored exam include having a post-secondary education in a health-related field, such as medicine, nursing, laboratory technology, or public health.[22] Individuals with an RN, LPN/LVN, an associate degree in nursing, or a Bachelor of Science in public health would be eligible.

Dr. Patricia Stone believes that nursing homes need their own targeted certification separate from the hospitals.

"For example, in hospitals, you don't have to worry as much about 'life safety' issues like leaving out cleaning agents for fear that a resident may eat it," she said.

Alongside IP certification, nursing home IPs desperately need IP collaboratives and mentoring opportunities. APIC state chapters are excellent for this community support; however, many states tend to have a heavy acute care focus, often leaving nursing home IPs feeling disconnected.

When I was the 2019 Arizona APIC Chapter President, I did everything in my power to create a platform for nursing homes, but attendance was dismal. Many nursing home IPs don't have leadership support to pay for the $220 APIC membership or the opportunity to attend monthly meetings.

On the other hand, Gwen reported that the Wisconsin Department of Health had great success with nursing home attendance at the Wisconsin State APIC chapter.

"We broke out into groups at one point in our meeting, and the nursing homes had a huge nursing home section. We'd discuss the problems of the day, and surveyors were there to answer questions. It was active and, in fact, some of the LTC people became officers and presidents and would rotate through," Gwen said.

The success of the Wisconsin APIC chapter gives me hope and encouragement to continue urging nursing homes to attend their local APIC chapter, as well as the public health and licensing division to offer active support and guidance for these emerging nursing home IPs.

When Doctors Without Borders has a field mission, they always aim to leave the community with an infrastructure that will enable the work to continue long after they've left.

The 2020 nursing home missions in Detroit and Houston were no exception. Understanding the need for nursing home-targeted IPC training, a "boots on the ground" program was created and left with various universities.[23] The program enables nursing students to learn IPC intricacies in nursing homes and promote and build up this unique profession.

Nursing homes can benefit tremendously from having access to this IPC toolkit, and students can use the experience to conduct capstone or thesis projects. By now it should be clear that having a proactive infection prevention and control program is essential to decreasing the harms and deaths associated from preventable infections. Now is the time to take this industry to the next level and build upon the foundation that has already been laid. Now is the time to provide the funding and support necessary to report HAI data into NHSN, invest in a full-time infection preventionist, and prioritize the funding for robust mentoring and training. If we are not deliberate about the next steps that we take, we will inevitably find ourselves in a similar situation in the future. Let's rally together and choose a different path. A path that saves lives, not disregards them because it costs too much money, or the road ahead is too hard.

Now, what are we going to do about the current punitive regulatory process?

CHAPTER 12

SURVEY REFORM

"We thought we were doing good; then we got a sixty-page report from an annual survey. Have you ever thought about how much trauma we have been through? I'm sorry that doesn't help.... The citations were for goofy paperwork that we missed here and there...more infection control surveys than we have ever had on top of everything. It was a lot."
—Anonymous Michigan nursing home administrator

I worked on-site in a Detroit nursing home. The resident population was active and packed with people in wheelchairs who lined the hallways. I said hello to a man who smiled big and laughed. Most of the residents appeared completely oblivious to the world around them. *Are they unaware?* I supposed this was why they required twenty-four-hour care in a nursing home. Shortly after I arrived, firefighters, paramedics, and police walked through the front door.

Stunned, I asked the infection preventionist what was going on.

"A resident has punched a worker," she said.

"Never a dull moment," I responded.

None of us ever want to think we'll spend our remaining years in a nursing home, as my grandparents Mee Mee and Dee Dee did. Or that we won't have sufficient assistance at home to help us rehabilitate from an injury, as happened with Lacy. In fact, most of us shudder at the thought, because nursing homes have such terrible reputations. We don't like them. The media doesn't like them, and the regulators believe the care is bad.

Now add a global pandemic to the mix of this already challenged, underfunded, and under-resourced healthcare environment, and you have a perfect catastrophic storm. The response? Apathy and disdain.

"We've seen ambivalence toward nursing homes for years," Dr. Konetzka told me. "Yet this pandemic was not in the nursing homes' control. Research came out showing that the virus was widespread in a nursing home when the community rates were high."

Dan, from Winslow Campus of Care, had already told me how CMS warned nursing homes at the onset of the pandemic: "Don't screw this up." And Katie Smith Sloan, CEO of the national nursing home advocacy group Leading Age, had said, "We've never had a virus before that was airborne and largely asymptomatic. Those two things alone create an almost impossible task of infection control as we are fighting this invisible enemy. The public health guidance was changing day by day, which shows you that there were no answers, and we were learning as we went. In the hospital, if something happens, it's an accident or mistake. In the nursing home, it's an infraction and an immediate jeopardy (IJ). Nursing homes have been unfairly maligned, and so many of them are doing such a fantastic job with such high stakes."

Nursing homes are currently more regulated than any other healthcare provider types, including hospitals and outpatient care settings.[1] There's constant legislative pressure to add more and more regulations and rules to ensure that appropriate care is being delivered. Meanwhile, enforcement of these regulations is ineffective and broken.

Part of the problem is that the surveyors, as Sylvia described, aren't appropriately trained. Whether a nursing home gets tagged depends on which surveyor is in the facility. "The survey process is now very much automated," she told me, "with the surveyors walking around with their laptops, looking for little nitpicky items. The team of surveyors is assigned different areas in the nursing homes to review, such as infection control, antibiotic stewardship, and life safety. The surveyor, depending on their background, timeline, comfort level, and interest can choose to dig deep or brush over a topic. Nobody is going to know the difference unless there's a federal surveyor observing them."

"Usually," she said, "they don't have time to evaluate all the issues as they only have a certain number of hours to complete the survey—and that can include traveling to and from the nursing home."

Given these constraints, this crunched time frame lends itself to a cookie-cutter approach, and what is often referred to as a "gotcha" mentality. The surveyors don't have the opportunity to sit down and work with a facility or offer assistance.

"If something was pretty small, we gave technical assistance and some advice," Sylvia said. "That just doesn't exist anymore."

I never thought a licensing agency would dictate my professional recommendations. But during this pandemic, I've found myself more often telling the nursing home staff to follow certain protocols, even if they don't make sense or contradict each other, to avoid a state citation.

This subjective mindset is pervasive across the country. Josh, the Idaho administrator, described how some nursing homes continue operating based on a citation they received twenty-five years ago.

"Why is your dietary manager changing the oil in your bus?" he asked, offering an exaggerated example. "Oh, well, twenty-five years ago we got tagged for it, so now this is what we do."

He's right. In the nursing home I helped Josh with, they had gotten a citation years prior for having alcohol-based hand-sanitizing dispensers in the hallway. Their response was to never put them up again, even though this is now a CDC recommendation.

There's also a fear component, Josh said. When you get a citation or a tag, it's a big deal that affects the facility's reputation.

"You're clearly not going to do that again to avoid getting into trouble," he continued. "But the opposite effect can be true as well. If a surveyor skims over everything without drawing appropriate attention to issues, then the nursing home believes they're doing well."

Before COVID-19, when I was offering nursing homes support to improve their infection prevention and control program, I heard time and time again, "No, we don't need any assistance, our state survey was good." These nursing homes, based on their survey, truly believed they were good with their program. Given the catastrophic nature of COVID-19 in this healthcare setting, we can venture to say they were not okay, regardless of what their state survey said.

Over time, as a solution to one or two incompetent nursing homes that make national news, the survey process has become bigger, stronger, and more in-depth. The more in-depth it gets, the harder it is for the nursing homes to comply or for the surveyors to be competently trained to regulate a facility appropriately.

Over-regulation tends to support the crisis mentality previously discussed: "Snap, fix this, no, go fix this," and "Whack-a-mole over here because the surveyors are coming." Is this overregulated system driving good people away from the industry?

"It's pretty difficult to maintain good MDs in the field," Josh told me. "I can't tell you how many doctors I've seen argue with surveyors. The surveyor may be a registered dietician and argue with a medical doctor with twenty years' experience, claiming they didn't write an order correctly. In what world is that okay?"

We need to return to implementing evidence-based practices and get away from a system driven by surveyor opinions. I was recently in a nursing home where the staff cut the straps to their N95 respirators and wore surgical masks over them to hold them up. The proper process is to have both straps pulled around to the back of the head to keep the respirator securely in place and offer the highest level of protection to the user. When I asked staff members why they cut the straps, they said the N95 respirators didn't fit them properly. The staff simply tried to comply with the infection control protocols while performing their job effectively.

I observed this problem at the same time that three state surveyors were in the building. Along with the IP, I went around instructing the staff on the appropriate process for wearing an N95 respirator and handing out new ones, but it was too late. The surveyors had seen them. We knew that this could result in a facility-wide infection control tag, which is the typical outcome.

Much to my surprise, that didn't happen. In fact, the nursing home didn't get any infection control tags. I was later told they were visited by the "easygoing" surveyors. This practice certainly isn't supporting a facility either. The infection control practices were clearly wrong and could potentially harm the healthcare workers, yet without a citation, the nursing home assumed they were doing everything right. I'm not even sure if the surveyors knew this was an improper practice.

Perhaps the nursing home was lucky that day. If they'd had a stricter surveyor, they might have been cited with an IJ. Consequently, when we let the survey process dictate our healthcare practices, we're operating on the surveyor's interpretation, not on research and evidence.

Early in my career, I worked with a wound nurse in a nursing home and noticed that she didn't wash her hands after removing a dirty wound dressing. She said the last nurse told her she only had to wash her hands before and after the wound care. This was clearly wrong. After removing a dirty dressing, nurses had to wash their hands to avoid contaminating the clean area. Can you imagine being operated on by a surgeon who conducts medical procedures based on the way their regulatory division grades them? What if their regulatory division had little to no training in surgical practices? Whatever the survey team says, or doesn't say, is how the nursing home operates. This is dangerous.

Another terrible problem with the current regulatory process and the "gotcha" mentality is that surveys are typically done annually. As a result, it's common for the staff to follow the rules when the surveyors are in-house, but return to their practices when the surveyors are out of the building. For example, one nursing home I've worked with for over three years started tracking how compliant their staff was with washing their hands. We noticed when the survey team was in-house, handwashing compliance went up from 60 percent to 80 percent. Of course, this performance made the state and nursing home happy because they performed well, but what about the rest of the year? There wasn't much incentive to continue working on improving handwashing because they did so well with the state survey.

This reminds me of educational standardized testing. It's similar, except it isn't standardized but rather subjectively graded. The nursing home takes the test once a year, then are graded on it. If their staff performs well, they get a high mark and a pat on the back, and no further action is taken. If they perform poorly, they are cited and required to put a plan of correction together in ten days and made to fill out large piles of paperwork to demonstrate to the state that they've fixed the problem. But have they?

Katie Smith Sloan hopes that COVID-19 will serve as a wake-up call and that, as a country, we will begin to take a hard look at nursing home regulations. Right now, the focus is on punishment rather than improvement.

I wondered if the Civil Monetary Plenary (CMP) funds that a facility has to pay keeps this punitive process in play. Remember Josh's building was fined over $100,000 for their IJ, and the Kirkland nursing home in Washington was fined over $600,000. According to CMS, a portion of the monies are reinvested back to the state and may be used as grants by facilities, the health department, and private industry to improve the quality of resident care.[2]

"Anybody interested could apply to utilize the funds," Diane Eckles told me. "However, the feds are quite picky about what they'll approve, and the procurement process is a bit overwhelming. The project has to benefit several skilled nursing facilities, and for the most part it can't be a project that's been done before. It should be a proven educational process and is favorable if the project has been successfully completed in other states but new to the one applying."

What's more, the legislature only allocates a certain amount of funding each year. Diane said that in Arizona, the annual funding is $100,000, which compared to what's actually in the fund [undisclosed], isn't a lot.

> Every July, there's a fresh pot of $100,000. I think right now we have about $20,000 left for this fiscal year, and it goes back into the appropriation if it's not used. We're looking into getting more appropriated every year, but it goes before the budget committee, and I'm sure CMS will want the interest on the funds, so they're very stingy with it. It's

money our facilities have paid to CMP, so it should go back to the facilities and not be used as a funding source for interest.

So, where do we go from here? What needs to occur to repair this broken, punitive process? I've heard arguments on both sides of the fence, for and against the survey process, but one thing everyone seems to agree on is that the current program isn't working. If we minimize the survey, then how do we combat the "awful owners" who make money by skimping on critical operations like staffing needs?

The thought behind this is that heavy fines will hurt facilities financially, and they'll be forced to fix the problem. Is this process working, though? In my experience, it seems to hurt the staff working in the nursing homes trying to do the right thing every day, not the corporate leaders or shareholders who never step foot in the facility.

One question I often hear is why does the federal government oversee nursing home regulations instead of having a separate entity that's properly licensed and accredited? The Joint Commission (TJC) is the nation's oldest and largest standards-setting and accrediting body in healthcare, and the industry perceives TJC as treating hospital professionals like subject matter experts through a collaborative quality improvement-minded model, unlike the CMS "gotcha" attitude.[3]

One nursing home administrator told me, "We show up to work every day because we care about the residents, and we care about what we do. Yet, there's this tendency to fault us. Even the media gets a kick out of blaming the nursing homes."

We must shift this punitive, punishing environment to one of collaboration. What if, instead of going to war with the surveyors every day, we forged a partnership with them? Certain advocate groups will say there are plenty of organizations, such as the CMS quality improvement organizations (QIOs), that are there to be collaborative. Still, we need a regulatory division to point out the problems. I argue that with the current length of the regulations and the inadequate training of the surveyors, this simply isn't possible.

We also must ask ourselves how moral and ethical it's been to throw the hammer down on a vulnerable population and its critical workforce during a global crisis? Dr. Konetzka said, "In the middle of a crisis, providing monetary incentives for quality measures and citing nursing homes with deficiencies is not going to help residents survive. It's not going to help those residents *not* die from COVID. That timing is especially bad."

Dr. Patricia Stone agreed. "We need to change the narrative and paradigm, as there's a difference between being a teacher and being a proctor. The bottom line is we need accreditation and regulation reform. We need coaching, not bullying by the surveyors, who often deliberately try to trick the staff. I was on a national commission where some people said, 'Blow up nursing homes. Just blow them all up.'"

Katie Smith Sloan had some thoughts about improving the regulatory system. "It must focus on what we can do to improve quality through learning collaboratives and quality improvement. This has to come from CMS and trickle down to the states. The partnerships between CMS and the states have to be in lockstep. It's a huge ship to turn around, but it's essential. The people who live and work in these facilities deserve it. They don't deserve going to work every day wondering if they're going to get dinged for washing their hands for eighteen seconds instead of twenty."

We now have the responsibility to come in and lead past the pandemic. Nobody gets into long-term care because it's lucrative or glamourous. I believe that our frontline workers, particularly our nurses and CNAs, are called to this work. It takes a special kind of person to do it. The perspective needs to shift from "If we don't make them do the right thing, then they're not going to do it" to "Let's treat our staff like the professionals they are and give them the training tools needed to be successful."

Josh felt the same way. "There are a lot of easier jobs that I could do with my degree. But you know what? I like what I do. I like making people's lives better, especially our elders. They deserve it. They're the reason we have the opportunities we do."

CHAPTER 13

ADVOCATE FOR CHANGE

"If you believe in a cause, be willing to stand up for that cause with a million people or by yourself."
—Otis S. Johnson

This book opened with a description of the day I attended the family council meeting at Patuxent Health and Rehabilitation Center in Baltimore, Maryland, and met Nannie. On that day, I made a promise to do everything that I could to help the nursing home reduce their infectious disease outbreaks.

Now I will describe the help that would eventually come through the brave and unyielding actions of Twila Bridges, family council president, and how you can take an active role in advancing the care in the nursing home where your loved one lives. We are not helpless, and we do have a voice.

When he was five years old, Twila Bridges' son Joseph was diagnosed with a rare disorder called Mucopolysaccharide Disorder or MPS Syndrome, a rare genetic disorder that results in childhood dementia and causes fatal brain damage.[1] The type her son had was Sanfilippo Syndrome, also known as Type 3.

Twila's family hadn't heard of this genetic disorder until Joseph was five years old, as it's commonly misdiagnosed until a child is much older. For the first twelve years of Joseph's life, Twila's medical insurance provided her with in-home respite care, additional in-home support meant to provide a family with relief from the care of a sick or disabled family member. The respite worker can be a family member or friend; however, it can also be a professional home caregiver, as in Joseph's case.

Twila was conscientious of who provided her son with intimate care like bathing, changing, and feeding.

"For twelve years, I would never allow anyone to care for my son who I didn't know," she told me. "I worked with every single staff member to get comfortable with them before they were left alone with Joseph."

On Thanksgiving Day in 1992, the respite aide scheduled for in-home care didn't show up. Consequently, the agency sent over a temporary aide as a replacement, someone the family had never met. This individual physically abused Joseph, a devastating and earth-shattering blow to Twila and her family. To make matters worse, shortly after, Twila lost her health insurance. Instead of offering in-home respite support, Prince George County Special Education Division in Maryland opted to pay $100,000 to send Joseph to a residential school program in Langhorne, Pennsylvania, two hours away from Twila and her family.

Twila made the long, tedious journey up and down corridor ninety-five to visit Joseph every day for two years until he got sick and was hospitalized at the Children's Hospital in Philadelphia. Twila pleaded with the

County to allow her to bring her son back home to care for him as only a mother can, but they told her she didn't have a choice, that her only option was to keep him at the residential school.

Twila recalls saying, "What do you mean, I don't have a choice?"

"This is the best you're gonna get," someone working with the county told her.

Her response was that of any able-bodied mother: "I don't think so," as she packed Joseph up and took him to the Children's Hospital in Washington, DC, where he received further medical care.

Twila longed to have Joseph at home with her and asked the genetic physician if this was a possibility. Unfortunately, Joseph had gotten worse over the course of two years while he was away. He was no longer walking or talking and was only eating puréed food. The physician informed Twila that Joseph's condition would only worsen, and he needed round-the-clock medical care, something Twila's family couldn't provide. His recommendation was to place fifteen-year-old Joseph in a nursing home. Twila was devastated by this news but knew that this was what was best for Joseph. At least he would be close to home, not two hours away.

Twila was provided a list of licensed nursing homes that could provide the essential care Joseph required. The options were limited given Joseph's age and condition. He lived at Crownsville Nursing Home, twenty minutes away from Twila, for two years, until he got sick again and was hospitalized for more than a month. He was then transferred to Mariner Health, now Patuxent Health and Rehabilitation Center, only a two-minute drive from where Twila lived.

Joseph remained there for twenty-two and half years until his passing on April 30, 2020. As a result of his residency in a facility, Twila had a unique view of nursing homes during the early onset of COVID-19, living at the bedside of her beloved son, night and day.

On March 13, 2020, a CMS newsroom press release announced that nursing homes were required to restrict all visitors, effective immediately, except for compassionate care visits.[2] Given Joseph's declining health, Twila was able to come into the facility to care for her son under those compassionate care guidelines. Hundreds and thousands of families and visitors would not be so fortunate.

"I remember the nurses came in and said there was a new CMS rule that required them to put a mask on the patient," Twila said. "Can you imagine doing this with no explanation to somebody with dementia? So, I had to explain to Joseph, you know, the reason why he had to have a mask on."

Twila noticed that the facility didn't have PPE supplies. "The staff was bringing in their own supplies, their own masks, their own face shields. They were being told to put on hospital gowns, the patient bed gowns, before they could get the disposable ones. They were handing out one per person and told they had to use it for their whole shift, then take it off and put it in their locker and use the same one the next day. You're not supposed to do that, right?"

Twila thought that she was doing better at following the CMS guidelines than the facility. "They were struggling with wiping down the high touch areas. I said, 'Give me a box of Clorox wipes!' They gave me whatever I needed. I was changing his dressing because the staff wasn't coming in. So, I would be like, 'God, go ahead and, you know, I'll turn him, I'll bathe him.' I did it all."

Twila's description of low PPE supplies was evident across the entire industry. The mandate to remove all visitors, along with the staff getting sick and quitting out of fear of the virus, left the resident population extremely vulnerable.

"They weren't getting the care," Twila said. "You can't have twelve to thirteen residents to one staff. Then it got to the point during COVID where they [staff] weren't coming to work. So, one night, there was nobody for the 3:00 p.m. to 11:00 p.m. shift, and they were pulling people from other units. It hurt me to see the distress on them. There were some nights I sat with Joseph until the next shift, the 11:00 p.m. to 7:00 a.m. shift."

One night in April of 2020, Twila received word that one of the nursing home residents had tested positive for COVID-19, as had two staff members. Joseph was the third resident to test positive.

"I went into his room the next night and said, 'You guys don't see him burning up?' His doctor was there, and the nurse ordered antibiotics and vitamin C, but it was too late for Joseph. They couldn't even get the antibiotic."

The facility ordered a chest X-ray that day and then another the following day. There was an obvious difference from the original X-ray that indicated some type of pneumonia or infection in Joseph's lungs. The nurse called 911 and he was transported to the closest hospital. Twila could only sit in the parking lot of the emergency room, separated from her son and powerless to help. Visitors were not allowed inside the ER.

Once he was stable—given Joseph's do-not-resuscitate status, the hospital wanted to send him to Glen Burnie, a nursing home that was accepting COVID-19 residents. His mother intervened.

"Twila said, 'No, I'm not sending him somewhere else to a facility who doesn't know him. It ain't the same. He'll stay where he's at!"

Having served as the Family Council President for years, Twila had connections to the State Senator's office, so she called the delegate's office, as well as the president of the hospital. She was told to change Joseph's DNR status to a full code to enable him to remain in the hospital.

"So that's what I did," Twila recalled. "That's how he was able to get through the weekend. But he was struggling, and come that Monday, his feeding tube burst, leaving him without nutrition, and his body was breaking down so bad the nurses struggled to get an IV in him. At that point, I told the doctor that we would not put him on a ventilator, but instead put him on morphine to keep him comfortable. He spent the last seven days without me, but I was connected with him through Zoom. Joseph died when he was forty years, eight months, and seven days. Yeah, that's my number, forty, eight, seven."

The reason for my visit to Patuxent Health and Rehabilitation Center that cold day on November 18, 2018, where I met Nannie, was to identify if there was an opportunity to support the facility with infection prevention and control protocols. The facility was in poor shape with infectious outbreaks and a leadership team unwilling to take action to mitigate the problems. Prior to this meeting, Twila, along with others at the Family Council meeting, had been deeply engaged with their local ombudsman, an advocate for nursing home residents who assists in resolving issues related to their health, safety, welfare, and nursing home rights. They were also deeply engaged with the Maryland Department of Health, Office of Health Care Quality (OHCQ) regulatory division, the Maryland State delegate, Joseline Peña-Melnyk, and the Maryland State Senator, Jim Rosapepe.

Twila and two other family members had a meeting with Delegate Peña-Melnyk and the OHCQ staff in September 2018. They were summoned back in November 2018 to meet with Senator Rosapepe and the nursing home's CEO. Twila recalled the CEO becoming hostile and defensive during the meeting, saying, "We should have known about these problems prior to the meeting."

This outburst shocked Twila because the CEO had previously been made aware of the complaints, as was the nursing home administrator who was sitting right next to him. In fact, it would have been a lot easier for them to help correct the issues before escalating the situation all the way to the state Senator's office.

"Well, you know what, this is—these folks here are my constituents," Senator Rosapepe said at that meeting, "and I don't see a reason why they would be sitting here today having to tell a lie." Twila listened as he went on to say, "I would expect, one year from now, this matter to be cleaned up and resolved."

Those were the last words that Twila remembers him saying that day. Soon after, the CEO brought his management team from corporate headquarters in Atlanta into the nursing home to examine what was going on. The VP of operations, Administrator, and DON quit or were terminated not long after.

Twila's brave journey advocating for quality, long-term care services for her son over two decades is helping guide the industry into the future. Her tenacity in fighting for Joseph and other nursing home residents is paving the way for other family and resident advocates. As US citizens, we should expect a high level of care delivered to our loved ones in nursing homes because it's taxpayer dollars that are being used.

"You're spending folks' money," Twila pointed out, "and you're treating them like they're an afterthought, you're treating them like dirt, you're treating them like they're not worthy anymore—especially those who have paid their dues to society, a lot of military folks. They'll say to you, 'Be thankful that you've got the place you got,'" Twila said.

This is the mentality Twila was up against and why she continues to fight so hard. Every person should be treated with respect and given quality care, no matter their medical condition.

Her success has proven that resident family members and patient advocates have a role in staying connected to senators, ombudsmen, AHCA/NCAL, state health departments, and organizations like Leading Age, and the Consumer Voice. Twila recommends a clear, firm message that you're paying attention. "I might be lean and small, but I'm not going away."

In February 2021, as an advocate for change, Twila testified before the House committee, telling her story and describing her nursing home experience. She made it known that staffing was the biggest problem before and during the COVID-19 pandemic, that there were times when the nursing homes didn't have anybody scheduled to work. Without the staff, there isn't anyone to change and reposition a resident, they're forced to sit in soiled briefs all day or sacrifice regular bathing, which leads to skin breakdown.

These are things that Twila experienced with Joseph. "I went in one day and he was in the same diaper from that morning. When I went in, it was 8:00 a.m. That evening at about 6:00 p.m., the diaper was soaked. How many other residents did this happen to?"

Twila was also asked to testify by delegate Mary Lehman to help get HR 983 passed. This is an emergency bill, not only for COVID-19, but in the event that a pandemic happens again. It enables a designated person or family member to be present for a nursing home resident. Twila testified, sharing her son's situation and how critical it was for her to be at his bedside every day. The bill passed in the house unanimously, went on to pass at the state level, and at the time of this writing is awaiting the governor's signature.[3]

Twila told me her experience with nursing homes wasn't all dreary and painful. They did provide the essential life-sustaining care that Joseph needed. But her active involvement with Joseph's care team was crucial. She never missed a care plan meeting that outlined the treatment he'd receive, and it was in these planning meetings that all concerns were raised, including those about the care the staff was providing.

Unfortunately, family members don't always get involved in their loved one's care. I don't know if families were invited to attend the care plan meeting in 1994 when Mee Mee and Dee Dee were in the nursing home, because I never got an invitation. I didn't know there was an ombudsman, or a family council meeting. I didn't know what I didn't know, and I blindly trusted.

This doesn't have to be a family member's experience. Involvement in the resident care plan of a loved one and participation in quarterly planning and review of the health and nursing care protocols can make a huge difference.[4]

Getting involved is key; we can't simply put our loved ones in a nursing home and then leave them there.

Twila and I remain in contact to support one another on this journey. "You plan on coming out here to Capitol Hill?" she asked me recently. "I see us going up to, you know, to Capitol Hill, with my picture on my shirt, my flag, whatever I need, you know, and now we fight the fight. But understand this: Many, many family members must journey with us. We need to increase in numbers; it needs to come from all across the country. We can really make a bigger impact."

* * *

This fight is in California. This fight is in New York. It is all across the country. It's not isolated to one place; it's national. At what point is enough, enough? The stories are all very much the same. I hope this book has told the story—the *true* story—behind the doors of our nursing homes and why they struggle as they do. Why the staff can't provide the high level of care that is needed. Why the time, like never before, is *now* to create change.

We need to advocate for more staffing, for a living wage for our frontline workers, for collaborative support instead of the nitpicky "gotcha" attitudes of the current regulatory process. We must partner with our nursing homes and advocate for the dedicated workers who get up every day to ensure our vulnerable loved ones live out their years with beauty and grace.

* * *

On July 22, 2021, I received an email from Crystal, Nannie's niece.

"Nannie passed on April 27," Crystal wrote. "She loved me unconditionally, and I loved her so much. I miss her and often wake up thinking that I am going to visit her that day or thinking about what I will take her to eat. My heart is broken."

EPILOGUE

COVID-19 did not cause the issues addressed in this book. This global pandemic has merely been the catalyst for the world to see a broken healthcare system in dire need of repair. If we don't take action now while we are awake and aware, then we will go back to "business as usual."

I am already starting to see this in many nursing homes.

Infection preventionists are once again being pulled to work the floor instead of being dedicated to the infection prevention and control program. Infection control practices—such as handwashing, wearing the appropriate personal protective equipment such as gowns, the appropriate process for cleaning and disinfecting the environment of care—are becoming lax again.

These are issues that will continue long into the future if we don't take action now and demand change.

It is my hope and prayer that this book has inspired you to take action, whether your loved one is in a nursing home or not. Chances are that someday you will need this kind of care. I've supplied resources that can support you in taking action. Please use and share these resources. Even if you don't have a lot of time, small steps collectively can set into motion lasting changes.

I reflect about my Mee Mee and Dee Dee and know that they have guided me through this journey. I have a picture of Dee Dee when he was only twenty-seven years old that I keep with me. He was so handsome with his dark black hair and infectious smile. I'll keep doing the work for him and Mee Mee...and for all of your loved ones.

Please. Will you join me in this effort?

For more information, visit *ipcwell.com/consumer-resources*.

ACKNOWLEDGMENTS

Without my dear friend Don encouraging me, I would not have been brave enough to write the nursing home stories that I witnessed across the country during the COVID-19 outbreak. Thank you for lighting a fire to write it with the urgency that it deserved.

To my large and extended family and friends for supporting my efforts on the road away from you. To Meagan for your unyielding effort to keep me organized and the countless hours of research and transcription that sparked this book to life. To my editors Jessica, Brian, Mary, Robrt, and Julia, this book would not be the same without your brilliance. To Tony, the Felice Agency team, and Scribe Media, your brilliant work will ensure that this story is deliberately told. To Dr. Peter Patterson, Dr. Kate Ellingson, and Dr. Connie Mariano for your support and guidance. To the brave individuals that were willing to tell their story, whether through a formal interview or simply in the hallway of a nursing home. It is through your stories that this book took on a life of its own.

To all the healthcare workers and staff that get up every day and continue to work in a challenging environment because you care for our loved ones when we can't. To the often unrecognized and underappreciated staff—the nurses, nursing aides, housekeepers, kitchen staff, social workers, and maintenance staff—may you be supported and valued every day.

Finally, to the residents. May you live out the remainder of your days with dignity and grace. May you be afforded the best healthcare in the safest environment possible because you matter, and you deserve it. With much love and prayers, Buffy.

NOTES

INTRODUCTION

1 U.S. Department of Health and Human Services, "Chapter 8: Long-Term Care Facilities," in *National Action Plan to Prevent Health Care-Associated Infection: Road Map to Elimination* (2013), 194–239, https://health.gov/sites/default/files/2019-09/hai-action-plan-ltcf.pdf

2 Lauren Harris-Kojetin et al., "Long-term Care Providers and Services Users in the United States, 2015–2016," *National Center for Health Statistics: Vital and Health Statistics* series 3, no. 43 (2019), https://www.cdc.gov/nchs/data/series/sr_03/sr03_43-508.pdf

3 Jeneita Bell, "Infection Surveillance and Prevention in Long-Term Care: A National Perspective" (National Healthcare Safety Network training, March 20, 2017), https://www.cdc.gov/nhsn/pdfs/training/2017/Bell_March20.pdf

4 Department of Health and Human Services, Office of Inspector General, *Adverse Events in Skilled Nursing Facilities: National Incidence Among Medicare Beneficiaries* by Daniel R. Levinson, https://oig.hhs.gov/oei/reports/oei-06-11-00370.pdf

CHAPTER 1

1 Blaizie Goveas, "Urosepsis: A Simple Infection Turns Toxic," *The Nurse Practitioner* 42, no. 7 (July 15, 2017): 53–54, https://doi.org/10.1097/01.npr.0000520425.91534.b8

CHAPTER 3

1 Laura Mills, "US: Concerns of Neglect in Nursing Homes," Human Rights Watch, March 25, 2021, https://www.hrw.org/news/2021/03/25/us-concerns-neglect-nursing-homes

2 Harris-Kojetin et al., "Long-term Care Providers."

3 *Nursing Home Reform: Continued Attention is Needed to Improve Quality of Care in Small but Significant Share of Homes, Before the Special Committee on Aging, U.S. Senat*e, 110th Cong., (2007) (statement of Kathryn G. Allen, Health Care Director), https://www.aging.senate.gov/imo/media/doc/hr172ka.pdf

4 Janet Rehnquist, Department of Health and Human Services, Office of Inspector General, *Quality Assurance Committees in Nursing Homes*, by Janet Rehnquist, OEI-01-01-00090: (2003), https://oig.hhs.gov/oei/reports/oei-01-01-00090.pdf

5 "Five-Star Quality Rating System," American Healthcare Association, accessed January 17, 2022, https://www.ahcancal.org/Survey-Regulatory-Legal/Pages/FiveStar.aspx

6 Center for Medicare & Medicaid Services, "Quality Measures," CMS.gov, last modified January 4, 2022, https://www.cms.gov/Medicare/Quality-Initiatives-Patient-Assessment-Instruments/NursingHomeQualityInits/NHQIQualityMeasures#5

7 Center for Medicare & Medicaid Services, "Five-Star Quality Rating System," CMS.gov (October 7, 2019), https://www.cms.gov/Medicare/Provider-Enrollment-and-Certification/CertificationandComplianc/FSQRS

8 Patient Protection and Affordable Care Act, H.R. 3590, 111th Cong. (2010), https://www.congress.gov/111/plaws/publ148/PLAW-111publ148.pdf

9 "HAI Action Plan," HHS.gov, accessed January 14, 2022, https://www.hhs.gov/oidp/topics/health-care-associated-infections/hai-action-plan/index.html

10 U.S. Department of Health and Human Services, "Chapter 8: Long-Term Care Facilities."

11 Centers for Disease Control and Prevention, "2019 AR Threats Report," CDC.gov, accessed January 17, 2022, https://www.cdc.gov/drugresistance/biggest-threats.html#cdiff8

12 "Medicare and Medicaid Programs; Reform of Requirements for Long-Term Care Facilities," 81 Fed. Reg. 68,688 (October 4, 2016), https://www.federalregister.gov/documents/2016/10/04/2016-23503/medicare-and-medicaid-programs-reform-of- requirements-for-long-term-care-facilities

13 "Health Services Advisory Group, Inc.," YouTube, 2018, https://www.youtube.com/user/hsagvideo.

14 Patricia W. Stone et al., "The Expansion of National Healthcare Safety Network Enrollment and Reporting in Nursing Homes: Lessons Learned from a National Qualitative Study," *American Journal of Infection Control* 47, no. 6 (March 5, 2019): 615–622, https://doi.org/10.1016/j.ajic.2019.02.005

CHAPTER 4

1 Centers for Disease Control and Prevention, Nimalie Stone, MD, https://blogs.cdc.gov/safehealthcare/bios/nimalie-stone-md/

2 U.S. Department of Health and Human Services, CDC, *Antibiotic Resistance Threats in the United States: 2019*. Atlanta, GA: U.S. Department of Health and Human Services, CDC, 2019. https://www.cdc.gov/drugresistance/pdf/threats-report/2019-ar-threats-report-508.pdf

3 "Nursing Homes and Assisted Living (Long-Term Care Facilities [LTCFs])," CDC.gov, accessed January 17, 2022, https://www.cdc.gov/longtermcare/index.html

4 Christine Kilgore, "COVID-19 Drives Nursing Homes to Overhaul Infection Control Efforts," MDedge.com, June 10, 2020, https://www.mdedge.com/chestphysician/article/223619/coronavirus-updates/covid-19-drives-nursing-homes-overhaul-infection

5 Lona Mody and Sandro Cinti, "Pandemic Influenza Planning in Nursing Homes: Are We Prepared?" *Journal of the American Geriatrics Society* 55, no. 9 (June 29, 2007): 1431–1437, https://doi.org/10.1111/j.1532-5415.2007.01299.x

6 Hannah Stower and Marianne Guennot, "Art in a Pandemic: A Digital Gallery," *Nature Medicine*, March 15, 2021, https://www.nature.com/articles/d41591-021-00009-5

7 *Caring for Seniors Amid the COVID-19 Crisis, Before the United States Senate Special Committee on Aging, U.S. Senate*, 116th Cong. (2020) (testimony of R. Tamara Konetzka, Professor University of Chicago), https://www.aging.senate.gov/imo/media/doc/SCA_Konetzka_05_21_20.pdf

8 "Infection Control Surveys at Nursing Facilites: CMS Data Not Plausible," Center for Medicare Advocacy, MedicareAdvocacy.org, June 11, 2020, https://medicareadvocacy.org/infection-control-surveys-at-nursing-facilities-cms-data-not-plausible/

CHAPTER 5

1 The New York Times, "Nearly One-Third of U.S. Coronavirus Deaths are Linked to Nursing Homes," *The New York Times*, last updated June 1, 2021, https://www.nytimes.com/interactive/2020/us/coronavirus-nursing-homes.html
2 Centers for Disease Control and Prevention, "SARS Basics Fact Sheet," CDC.gov, January 13, 2004, https://www.cdc.gov/sars/about/fs-sars.html
3 Ilene Warner-Maron, "A Look Inside: *60 Minutes* Reveals Early Struggles a LTC Facility Faced in the Wake of COVID-19," November 5, 2020, https://www.hmpgloballearningnetwork.com/site/altc/content/look-inside-60-minutes-reveals-early-struggles-ltc-facility-faced-wake-covid-19
4 Director Quality, Safety & Oversight Group to State Survey Agency Directors, memorandum, "Revised COVID-19 Survey Activities, CARES Act Funding, Enhanced Enforcement for Infection Control Deficiencies" (January 4, 2021), QSO-20-31-All, https://www.cms.gov/files/document/qso-20-31-all- revised.pdf
5 CDC Newsroom, "HHS Delivers Funding to Expand Testing Capacity for States, Territories, Tribes," press release, CDC.gov, May 18, 2020, https://www.cdc.gov/media/releases/2020/p0518-hhs-funding-expand-testing-states.html
6 CDC Newsroom, "HHS Delivers Funding."

CHAPTER 6

1 "Who We Are," Médicins Sans Frontières, accessed January 17, 2022, https://www.msf.org/who-we-are
2 "Clean Hands Count: Prevent and Control Infections Overview," CMS.gov, accessed January 17, 2022, https://www.cms.gov/files/document/hand-hygiene-initiative-overview.pdf
3 Proverbs 1:8–10 (NIV), https://www.biblegateway.com/passage/?search=Proverbs%2031:8-10&version=NIV
4 Centers for Disease Control and Prevention, "Interim Infection Prevention and Control Recommendations to Prevent SARS-CoV-2 Spread in Nursing Homes," CDC.gov, last updated September 10, 2021, https://www.cdc.gov/coronavirus/2019-ncov/hcp/long-term-care.html

CHAPTER 7

1 Centers for Medicare & Medicaid Services, "Exhibit 7A: Principles of Documentation," in *State Operations Manual,* 100–007, accessed January 17, 2022, https://www.cms.gov/Regulations-and-Guidance/Guidance/Manuals/downloads/som107_exhibit_007a.pdf

2 Jonathan Lips, "MDH Addresses Questions on Directed Plans of Correction to Nursing Homes," LeadingAge Minnesota, February 3, 2021, https://www.leadingagemn.org/news/mdh-addresses-questions-on-directed-plans-of-correction-to-nursing-homes/

3 E. Tammy Kim, "This Is Why Nursing Homes Failed So Badly," *The New York Times*, December 31, 2021, https://www.nytimes.com/2020/12/31/opinion/sunday/covid-nursing-homes.html?searchResultPosition=1

4 Centers for Disease Control and Prevention, "Post-COVID Conditions: Information for Healthcare Providers," CDC.gov, July 9, 2021, https://www.cdc.gov/coronavirus/2019-ncov/hcp/clinical-care/post-covid-conditions.html

5 Director Survey and Certification Group to State Survey Agency Directors, memorandum, "Interim Final Rule (IFC), CMS-3401-IFC, Additional Policy and Regulatory Revisions in Response to the COVID-19 Public Health Emergency related to Long-Term Care (LTC) Facility Testing Requirements," September 10, 2021, QSO-20-38-NH, https://www.cms.gov/files/document/qso-20-38-nh-revised.pdf

6 Texas Health and Human Services, "Nursing Facility CMS-Mandated COVID-19 Testing Frequently Asked Questions," HHS.Texas.gov, https://www.hhs.texas.gov/sites/default/files/documents/services/health/coronavirus-covid-19/nf-cms-mandated-covid-testing-faqs.pdf

7 Centers for Disease Control and Prevention, "Interim Infection Prevention."

CHAPTER 8

1 Centers for Medicaid & Medicare Services, "Nursing Homes," CMS.gov, last updated December 7, 2021, https://www.cms.gov/Medicare/Provider-Enrollment-and-Certification/CertificationandComplianc/NHs

2 The Henry J. Keiser Foundation, "Medicaid's Role in Nursing Home Care," June 2017, https://files.kff.org/attachment/Infographic-Medicaids-Role-in-Nursing-Home-Care

3 Centers for Medicaid and Medicare Services, "Nursing Homes."

4 CMS Newsroom, "Trump Administration Unveils Enhanced Enforcement Actions Based on Nursing Home COVID-19 Data and Inspection Results," press release, CMS.gov, June 1, 2020, https://www.cms.gov/newsroom/press-releases/trump-administration-unveils-enhanced-enforcement-actions-based-nursing-home-covid-19-data-and

5 Robert R. Redfield and Seema Verma to United States Governors, letter, May 31, 2020, https://www.cms.gov/files/document/6120-letter-governors.pdf

6 CMS Newsroom, "Trump Administration Unveils Enhanced."

7 CMS Newsroom, "Trump Administration Unveils Enhanced."

8 American Health Care Association and National Center for Assisted Living, "Timeline: COVID-19 and Nursing Homes," AHCANCAL.org, March 17, 2021, https://www.ahcancal.org/News-and-Communications/Fact-Sheets/FactSheets/Timeline-COVID-Nursing-Homes.pdf

9 Rebecca J. Gorges and R. Tamara Konetzka, "Staffing Levels and COVID-19 Cases and Outbreaks in U.S. Nursing Homes," *Journal of the American Geriatrics Society* 68, no. 11 (August 2020): 2462–2466, https://doi.org/10.1111/jgs.16787

10 *Caring for Seniors Amid the COVID-19 Crisis.*

11 *Caring for Seniors Amid the COVID-19 Crisis.*

12 Bill Whitaker for *60 Minutes*, "'No COVID-19 Tests Were Available': Inside the Country's First COVID-19 Outbreak," YouTube video, 13:24, November 1, 2020, https://www.youtube.com/watch?v=fPqHCcvP_cA

13 Maggie Flynn, "Verma Pushes Back on Criticism of CMS Response to Life Care COVID Outbreak: 'Our Inspection Was Critical,'" Skilled Nursing News, November 3, 2020, https://skillednursingnews.com/2020/11/verma-pushes-back-on-criticism-of-cms-response-to-life-care-covid-outbreak-our-inspection-was-critical/

14 Central District Health, "Central Idaho Healthcare Coalition" (2020), https://cdhd.idaho.gov/eh-hcc.php

15 CMS Newsroom, "Trump Administration Has Issued More than $15 Million in Fines to Nursing Homes During COVID-19 Pandemic," press release, CMS.gov, August 14, 2020, https://www.cms.gov/newsroom/press-releases/trump-administration-has-issued-more-15-million-fines-nursing-homes-during-covid-19-pandemic

16 CMS Newsroom, "Trump Administration Has Issued."

17 Maggie Flynn, "Infection Control Immediate Jeopardy Citations Tripled in 2020—and Nursing Homes Should Expect Even More," Skilled Nursing News, April

4, 2021, https://skillednursingnews.com/2021/04/infection-control-immediate-jeopardy-citations-tripled-in-2020-and-nursing-homes-should-expect-even-more/

CHAPTER 9

1 Centers for Disease Control and Prevention, "Transmission-Based Precautions, Example Signs (Posters)," CDC.gov, accessed January 17, 2022, https://www.cdc.gov/infectioncontrol/basics/transmission-based-precautions.html; Centers for Disease Control and Prevention, "Sequence for Putting On Personal Protective Equipment (PPE)," CDC.gov, last accessed January 17, 2022, https://www.cdc.gov/hai/pdfs/ppe/ppe-sequence.pdf
2 Centers for Disease Control and Prevention, "Interim Infection Prevention."

CHAPTER 10

1 The National Consumer Voice for Quality Long-Term Care, "The Devastating Effect of Lockdowns on Residents of Long-Term Care Facilities During COVID-19: A Survey of Residents' Families," National Consumer Voice for Quality Long-Term Care, January 15, 2021, https://theconsumervoice.org/uploads/files/issues/Devasting_Effect_of_Lockdowns_on_Residents_of_LTC_Facilities.pdf
2 Andrew D. Foster and Yong Suk Lee, "Staffing Subsidies and the Quality of Care in Nursing Homes," *Journal of Health Economics* 41 (Feb. 19, 2015): 133–147, https://dx.doi.org/10.1016%2Fj.jhealeco.2015.02.002
3 Charlene Harrington et al, "Appropriate Nurse Staffing Levels for U.S. Nursing Homes," *Health Services Insights* 13 (June 29, 2020): 1-14, https://www.ncbi.nlm.nih.gov/pmc/articles/PMC7328494/pdf/10.1177_1178632920934785.pdf
4 Alex Spanko, "75% of Nursing Homes 'Almost Never' in Compliance with RN Staffing Levels, Skilled Nursing News, July 1, 2019, https://skillednursingnews.com/2019/07/75-of-nursing-homes-almost-never-in-compliance-with-rn-staffing-levels/
5 Gorges and Konetzka, "Staffing Levels and COVID-19."
6 Coalition of Geriatric Nursing Organizations, "Nursing Staffing Requirements to Meet the Demands of Today's Long Term Care Consumer," American Nurse Association, November 12, 2014, https://www.nursingworld.org/practice-policy/nursing-excellence/official-position-statements/id/nursing-staffing-requirements-to-meet-the-demands-of-todays-long-term-care-consumer/

7 The National Consumer Voice for Quality Long-Term Care, "Better Staffing: The Key to Better Care," accessed January 17, 2022, https://theconsumervoice.org/betterstaffing

8 Paraprofessional Health Institute, "Raise the Floor: Quality Nursing Home Care Depends on Quality Jobs," PHI National, April 11, 2016, https://phinational.org/resource/raise-the-floor-quality-nursing-home-care-depends-on-quality-jobs/

9 Tanya Lewis, "Nursing Home Workers Had One of the Deadliest Jobs of 2020," *Scientific American*, February 18, 2021, https://www.scientificamerican.com/article/nursing-home-workers-had-one-of-the-deadliest-jobs-of-2020/

10 Will Englund, "In a Relentless Pandemic, Nursing-home Workers are Worn Down and Stressed Out," *The Washington Post*, December 3, 2020, https://www.washingtonpost.com/business/2020/12/03/nursing-home-burnout/

CHAPTER 11

1 Mayuko Uchida et. al, "Infection Prevention in Long-Term Care: A Systematic Review of Randomized and Nonrandomized Trials," *Journal of the American Geriatrics Society* 61, no. 4 (March 21, 2013): 602–614, https://doi.org/10.1111/jgs.12175

2 Association of Professionals in Infection Control and Epidemiology, "About APIC," APIC.org, accessed January 17, 2022, https://apic.org/about-apic/about-apic-overview/

3 Mola S. Donaldson, "Chapter 3: An Overview of *To Err Is Human*: Re-Emphasizing the Message of Patient Safety," in *Patient Safety and Quality: An Evidence-Based Handbook for Nurses*, ed. Ronda G. Hughes (Rockville, MD: Agency for Healthcare Research and Quality, 2008), https://www.ncbi.nlm.nih.gov/books/NBK2673/

4 Marilyn Hanchett, "The Infection Control Nurse: Approaching the End of an Era," *Infection Control Today*, August 31, 2015, https://www.infectioncontroltoday.com/view/infection-control-nurse-approaching-end-era

5 Francesca Torriani and Randy Taplitz, "Chapter 6: History of Infection Prevention and Control," in *Infectious Diseases*, 3rd ed., eds. Jonathan Cohen, Steven M. Opal, and William G. Powderly (Maryland Heights: Mosby, 2010), 76–85, https://www.ncbi.nlm.nih.gov/pmc/articles/PMC7151947/pdf/main.pdf

6 Centers for Disease Control and Prevention, "National Healthcare Safety Network (NHSN)", https://www.cdc.gov/nhsn/index.html

7 Catherine C. Cohen et al., "State Focus on Health Care-Associated Infection Prevention in Nursing Homes," *American Journal of Infection Control* 42, no. 2 (April 1, 2014): 360–365, https://doi.org/10.1016/j.ajic.2013.11.024
8 U.S. Department of Health and Human Services, "Part 2: Framework," in *National Action Plan to Prevent Health Care-Associated Infection: Road Map to Elimination* (2013), 20–40, https://health.gov/sites/default/files/2019-09/hai-action-plan-framework.pdf
9 Centers for Medicare & Medicaid Services, "Quality Improvement Organization (QUIO) 10th Statement of Work: Summary of Contract Results," AQAF.com, 2014, http://www.aqaf.com/10sow/results.pdf.
10 Carolyn T. A. Herzig et al., "State-Mandated Reporting of Health Care-Associated Infections in the United States: Trends Over Time," *American Journal of Medical Quality* 30, no. 5 (Sept.–Oct. 2015): 417–424, https://doi.org/10.1177/1062860614540200
11 Centers for Disease Control and Prevention, "2019 National and State Healthcare–Associated Infections Progress Report," CDC.gov, accessed January 17, 2022, https://www.cdc.gov/hai/data/archive/2019-HAI-progress-report.html#2018.
12 Centers for Disease Control and Prevention, "2019 National and State."
13 Director Quality, Safety & Oversight Group to State Survey Agency Directors, memorandum, "Interim Final Rule – COVID-19 Vaccine Immunization Requirements for Residents and Staff," May 11, 2021, QSO-21-19-NH, https://www.cms.gov/files/document/qso-21-19-nh.pdf
14 Director Quality, Safety & Oversight Group to State Survey Agency Directors, memorandum, "Interim Final Rule."
15 Wisconsin Department of Health Services, "Guidance for Preventing Transmission of Carbapenem-Resistant *Enterobacteriaceae* (CRE) in Acute Care and Long-Term Care Hospitals," DHS Wisconsin, May 2018, https://www.dhs.wisconsin.gov/publications/p0/p00532a.pdf; Wisconsin Department of Health Services, "Carbapenem-Resistant Enterobacterales (CRE)," DHS Wisconsin, accessed January 17, 2022, https://www.dhs.wisconsin.gov/disease/cre.htm
16 Centers for Disease Control and Prevention, "Carbapenem-Resistant Enterobacterales (CRE)," CDC.gov, accessed January 17, 2022, https://www.cdc.gov/hai/organisms/cre/index.html
17 Centers for Disease Control and Prevention, "Carbapenem-Resistant Enterobacterales (CRE)."

18 Association of Professionals in Infection Control and Epidemiology, "Who Are Infection Preventionists?" APIC.org, accessed January 17, 2022, https://apic.org/monthly_alerts/who-are-infection-preventionists/

19 "Medicare and Medicaid Programs; Requirements for Long-Term Care Facilities: Regulatory Provisions To Promote Efficiency, and Transparency," 84 Fed. Reg. 34,737 (July 18, 2019), https://federalregister.gov/d/2019-14946

20 Hanson Bridgett, Jillian Somers Donovan, and Lori Ferguson, "New California Law Imposes Additional Infection Preventionist and Reporting Requirements on Skilled Nursing Facilities," Hanson Bridgett, October 5, 2020, https://www.hansonbridgett.com/Publications/articles/2020-10-05-infection-preventionist-and-reporting-requirements#:~:text=Starting%20Jan.,direct%20patient%20care%20staffing%20calculations.

21 Richard Capparell, "Certification, A Defining Difference," handout, APIC.org, April 19, 2019, https://apic.org/wp-content/uploads/2019/07/Certification-Handout-4_19_19.pdf

22 Certification Board of Infection Control and Epidemiology, Inc., "About the CIC® Exam," CBIC.org, accessed January 17, 2022, https://www.cbic.org/CBIC/CIC-Certification/About-the-Examination.htm

23 Doctors Without Borders," IPC & Wellness Tool Kit Video Series," accessed January 17, 2022, https://www.doctorswithoutborders.org/IPCtoolkit

CHAPTER 12

1 Alyssa Gerace, "The Atlantic: Nursing Homes Still Operated Like Asylums, but They're Changing," Senior Housing News, May 29, 2012, https://seniorhousingnews.com/2012/05/29/the-atlantic-nursing-homes-still-operated-like-asylums-but-theyre-changing/

2 Centers for Medicare & Medicaid Services, "Civil Money Penalty Reinvestment Program," CMS.gov, last updated December 1, 2021, https://www.cms.gov/Medicare/Provider-Enrollment-and- Certification/SurveyCertificationGenInfo/LTC-CMP-Reinvestment

3 The Joint Commission, "70 Years of Patient Safety and Quality Healthcare," JointCommission.org, last accessed January 17, 2022, https://www.jointcommission.org/about-us/70-years-of-patient-safety-and-quality-healthcare/

CHAPTER 13

1 Genetics Home Reference, "Mucopolysaccharidosis Type III," MedlinePlus, last updated August 18, 2020, https://medlineplus.gov/genetics/condition/mucopolysaccharidosis-type-iii/

2 CMS Newsroom, "CMS Announces New Measures to Protect Nursing Home Residents from COVID-19," press release, CMS.gov, May 13, 2020, https://www.cms.gov/newsroom/press-releases/cms-announces-new-measures-protect-nursing-home-residents-covid-19

3 Nursing Homes – COVID-19 and Other Catastrophic Health Emergencies – Visitation (The Gloria Daytz Lewis Act), MD HB983, 441st session, May 30, 2021, https://www.billtrack50.com/BillDetail/1302902

4 Centers for Medicare & Medicaid Services, "What's a Care Plan in a Nursing Home?" Medicare.gov, accessed January 17, 2022, https://www.medicare.gov/what-medicare-covers/what-part-a-covers/whats-a-care-plan-in-a-nursing-home

GLOSSARY

Acute care hospital: a hospital that provides inpatient medical care and other related services for surgery, acute medical conditions, or injuries (usually for a short-term illness or condition). *www.cms.gov/Research-Statistics-Data-and-Systems/Research/ResearchGenInfo/Downloads/DataNav_Glossary_Alpha.pdf*

Airborne transmission: the spread of an infectious agent caused by the dissemination of droplet nuclei (aerosols) that remain infectious when suspended in air over long distances and time. *www.who.int/news-room/commentaries/detail/transmission-of-sars-cov-2-implications-for-infection-prevention-precautions*

Alcohol Based Hand Rub (ABHR): an alcohol-containing preparation (liquid, gel, or foam) designed for application to the hands to inactivate microorganisms and/or temporarily suppress their growth. Such preparations may contain one or more types of alcohol, other active ingredients with excipients, and humectants. *www.ncbi.nlm.nih.gov/books/NBK144046*

American Health Care Association (AHCA)/National Center for Assisted Living (NCAL): The American Health Care Association and the National Center for Assisted Living (AHCA/NCAL) is the largest association in the United States representing long term and post-acute care providers, with more than fourteen thousand member facilities. Their diverse membership includes non-profit and proprietary skilled nursing centers, assisted living communities, sub-acute centers, and homes for individuals with intellectual and development disabilities. By delivering solutions for quality care, AHCA/NCAL aims to improve the lives of the millions of the frail, elderly, and individuals with disabilities who receive long-term or post-acute care in our member facilities each day. *www.ahcancal.org/About/Pages/default.aspx*

American Recovery and Reinvestment Act of 2009 (ARRA): signed into law by President Barack Obama on February 17, 2009. It is an unprecedented effort to jumpstart our economy, create or save millions of jobs, and put a down payment on addressing long-neglected challenges so our country can thrive in the twenty-first century. *commonfund.nih.gov/arra*

Antibiotic stewardship: Antibiotic stewardship is the effort to measure and improve how antibiotics are prescribed by clinicians and used by patients. Improving antibiotic prescribing and use is critical to effectively treat infections, protect patients from harms caused by unnecessary antibiotic use, and combat antibiotic resistance. *www.cdc.gov/antibiotic-use/core-elements/index.html*

Antifungal medications/agents: a drug that selectively eliminates fungal pathogens from a host with minimal toxicity to the host. *www.ncbi.nlm.nih.gov/books/NBK8263*

Arthritis: the swelling and tenderness of one or more joints. The main symptoms of arthritis are joint pain and stiffness, which typically worsen with age. *www.mayoclinic.org/diseases-conditions/arthritis/symptoms-causes/syc-20350772*

Assistant Director of Nurses (ADON): responsible for the nursing team and quality of patient service in the absence of the director of nursing. The ADON supervises, analyzes, delegates, and evaluates nursing activities and ensures patient comfort and care. *www.betterteam.com/assistant-director-of-nursing-job-description*

Assisted living facility: Assisted living is for people who need help with daily care, but not as much help as a nursing home provides. Assisted living facilities range in size from as few as twenty-five residents to 120 or more. Typically, a few "levels of care" are offered, with residents paying more for higher levels of care. Assisted living residents usually live in their own apartments or rooms and share common areas. They have access to many services, including up to three meals a day; assistance with personal care; help with medications, housekeeping, and laundry; twenty-four-hour supervision, security, and on-site staff; and social and recreational activities. Exact arrangements vary from state to state. *www.nia.nih.gov/health/residential-facilities-assisted-living-and-nursing-homes*

Association for Professionals in Infection Control and Epidemiology (APIC): the leading professional association for infection preventionists (IPs) with more than fifteen thousand members. Their mission is to advance the science and practice of infection prevention and control. Most APIC members are nurses, physicians, public health professionals, epidemiologists, microbiologists, or medical technologists who collect, analyze, and interpret health data to track infection trends, plan appropriate interventions, measure success, and report relevant data to public health agencies; establish scientifically based infection prevention practices and collaborate with the healthcare team to assure implementation; work to prevent healthcare-associated infections (HAIs) in healthcare facilities by isolating sources of infections and limiting their transmission; educate healthcare personnel and the public about infectious diseases and how to limit their spread. *apic.org/about-apic/about-apic-overview*

Beneficiary and Family-Centered Care Quality Improvement Organizations (BFCC-QIO): helps people who have Medicare exercise their right to high-quality healthcare by managing all complaints and quality-of-care reviews to ensure consistency in the review process, handling cases in which Medicare patients want to appeal a healthcare provider's decision to discharge them from the hospital or discontinue other types of services, using the Immediate Advocacy process to address complaints quickly, and providing Health Care Navigation. *services. qioprogram.org/about/what-are-qios*

Bilevel Positive Airway Pressure (BiPAP): a type of ventilator—a device that helps with breathing. During normal breathing, your lungs expand when you breathe in; this is caused by the diaphragm, which is the main muscle of breathing in your chest, going in a downward direction. *www.hopkinsmedicine.org/health/treatment-tests-and-therapies/bipap*

Candida auris: Candida auris is an emerging fungus that presents a serious global health threat. The CDC is concerned about C. auris for three main reasons: It is often multidrug-resistant, meaning that it is resistant to multiple antifungal drugs commonly used to treat Candida infections. Some strains are resistant to all three available classes of antifungals. It is difficult to identify with standard laboratory methods, and it can be misidentified in labs without specific technology. Misidentification may lead to inappropriate management. It has caused outbreaks in healthcare settings. For this reason, it is important to quickly identify C. auris in a hospitalized patient so that healthcare facilities can take special precautions to stop its spread. *www.cdc.gov/fungal/candida-auris/index.html*

Carbapenem-Resistant Enterobacteriaceae (CRE): Enterobacterales are a large order of different types of germs (bacteria) that commonly cause infections in healthcare settings. Examples of germs in the Enterobacterales order include Escherichia coli (E. coli) and Klebsiella pneumoniae. *www.cdc.gov/hai/organisms/cre/index.html*

Catheter Associated Blood Stream Infections (CLABSI): a laboratory-confirmed bloodstream infection not related to an infection at another site that develops within forty-eight hours of a central line placement. Most cases are preventable with proper aseptic techniques, surveillance, and management strategies. *www.ncbi.nlm.nih.gov/books/NBK430891*

Catheter-Associated Urinary Tract Infections (CAUTI): A catheter-associated urinary tract infection (CAUTI) occurs when germs (usually bacteria) enter the urinary tract through the urinary catheter and cause infection. CAUTIs have been associated with increased morbidity, mortality, healthcare costs, and length of stay. The risk of CAUTI can be reduced by ensuring that catheters are used only when needed and removed as soon as possible; that catheters are placed using proper aseptic technique; and that the closed sterile drainage system is maintained. *www.cdc.gov/hai/ca_uti/cauti_faqs.html*

Centers for Disease Control and Prevention (CDC): serves as the national focus for developing and applying disease prevention and control, environmental health, and health promotion and health education activities designed to improve the health of the people of the United States. *www.cdc.gov/about/organization/cio-orgcharts/pdfs/CDCfs-508.pdf*

Centers for Medicare and Medicaid Services (CMS): provides health coverage to more than one hundred million people through Medicare, Medicaid, the Children's Health Insurance Program, and the Health Insurance Marketplace. The CMS seeks to strengthen and modernize the nation's healthcare system, to provide access to high-quality care and improved health at lower costs. *www.usa.gov/federal-agencies/centers-for-medicare-and-medicaid-services*

The Certification Board of Infection Control and Epidemiology, Inc. (CBIC): endorses the concept of voluntary, periodic certification for all infection prevention and control professionals meeting educational and practice requirements. The purpose of the certification process is to protect the public by providing standardized measurement of current basic knowledge needed for persons practicing infection prevention and control in all healthcare settings; encouraging individual growth and study, thereby promoting professionalism among infection prevention and control professionals; formally recognizing infection prevention and control professionals who fulfill the requirements for certification. *www.cbic.org/CBIC/Get-Certified.htm*

Certified Nursing Assistant (CNA): A certified nursing assistant helps patients with direct healthcare needs, often under the supervision of a nurse. Certified nursing assistants may also be called nursing assistants, nurse's aides, or patient care assistants. CNAs work directly with patients and nurses, helping with the many physical and complex tasks for patient care. *www.wgu.edu/blog/what-cna-job-description-career-guide2008.html#close*

Certification and Survey Provider Enhanced Reporting System (CASPER) data: an on-line data system from the Centers for Medicare and Medicaid Services (CMS). CASPER systems include data for all certified nursing facilities in the US. The data are collected in separate sets of files: (1) provider information, staffing data, and health information on residents; and (2) survey deficiencies. CASPER data from the annual surveys are combined with data from complaint surveys. *www.kff.org/report-section/nursing-facilities-staffing-residents-and-facility-deficiencies-2009-through-2016-appendix*

CIC Certification/Credential: The CIC® credential identifies healthcare professionals who have shown mastery in knowledge of infection prevention and control by sitting for and passing the certification exam. The CIC® credential shows a commitment to best practices in infection prevention and control and improved patient care and signals to your employer and colleagues that you are committed to your professional growth. *apic.org/education-and-events/certification*

CINTAS: supplier of corporate identity uniform programs, providing entrance and logo mats, restroom supplies, promotional products, first aid, safety, and fire protection products and services. *www.cintas.com/company*

Citrobacter: bacteria species are commonly found in water, soil, food, and the intestinal tracts of animals and humans. Many Citrobacter infections are nosocomially acquired; however, they can also be community acquired. A large surveillance study demonstrated that 0.8 percent of Gram-negative infection was caused by Citrobacter spp. In the hospital settings, Citrobacter spp. might account for 3 to 6 percent of all Enterobacteriaceae causing nosocomial infection. In patient with Citrobacter infections, the bacteria can be transmitted vertically from mother or horizontally from carriers or other hospital sources. The infection may occur as sporadic cases or nosocomial outbreaks. Vertical or nosocomial transmission may account for the origin of bacteria in some sporadic cases, and transmission from carriers such as family members or other contacts accounts for others. *www.antimicrobe.org/b93.asp*

Civil Monetary Penalty (CMP): A monetary penalty the Centers for Medicare & Medicaid Services (CMS) may impose against nursing homes for either the number of days or for each instance a nursing home is not in substantial compliance with one or more Medicare and Medicaid participation requirements for long-term care facilities. A portion of CMPs collected from nursing homes are returned to the states in which CMPs are imposed. State CMP funds may be reinvested to support activities that benefit nursing home residents and that protect or improve their quality of care or quality of life. *www.cms.gov/Medicare/Provider-Enrollment-and-Certification/SurveyCertificationGenInfo/LTC-CMP-Reinvestment*

Clostridioides difficile: a bacterium that causes an infection of the large intestine (colon). Symptoms can range from diarrhea to life-threatening damage to the colon. *www.mayoclinic.org/diseases-conditions/c-difficile/symptoms-causes/syc-20351691*

Coronavirus Aid, Relief, and Economic Security (CARES) Act: passed by Congress on March 27, 2020. This bill allotted $2.2 trillion to provide fast and direct economic aid to the American people negatively impacted by the COVID-19 pandemic. *www2.ed.gov/about/offices/list/ope/caresact.html*

CMS federal survey: Nursing home surveys are conducted in accordance with survey protocols and Federal requirements to determine whether a citation of non-compliance appropriate. The survey protocols and interpretive guidelines serve to clarify and/or explain the intent of the regulations. All surveyors are required to use them in assessing compliance with Federal requirements. Deficiencies are based on violations of the regulations, which are to be based on observations of the nursing home's performance or practices. *www.cms.gov/Medicare/Provider-Enrollment-and-Certification/GuidanceforLawsAndRegulations/Nursing-Homes*

CMS Quality Improvement Network-Quality Improvement Organizations (QIN-QIO): QIN-QIOs bring Medicare beneficiaries, providers, and communities together in data-driven initiatives that increase patient safety, make communities healthier, better coordinate post-hospital care, and improve clinical quality. QIN-QIOs are skilled in creating opportunities for providers to learn from each other, applying advanced improvement and analytical methods, engaging patients and families, and structuring processes for sustaining positive change. QIN-QIOs serve regions of two to six states, which means best practices for better care spread more quickly, while still accommodating local conditions and cultural factors. *www.cms.gov/Medicare/Quality-Initiatives-Patient-Assessment-Instruments/QualityImprovementOrgs/Downloads/Fact-Sheet-Quality-Innovation-Network-%E2%80%94-Quality-Improvement-Organizations-QIN-QIOs.pdf*

CMS-2567: statement of deficiencies and plan for correction. *www.cms.gov/Medicare/cms-Forms/cms-Forms/downloads/cms2567.pdf*

Coalition of Geriatric Nursing Organizations and the American Nursing Association (CGNO): is comprised of the leading associations representing nurses who provide geriatric care in a variety of clinical settings. By leveraging its collective strengths, CGNO speaks with one voice to promote a healthcare environment for older adults that reflect accessibility, evidence-based practice, and high-quality, person-centered care. *eldercareworkforce.org/coalition-of-geriatric-nursing-organizations*

Contact transmission: the most common form of transmitting diseases and viruses. There are two types of contact transmission: direct and indirect. Direct contact transmission occurs when there is physical contact between an infected person and a susceptible person. Indirect contact transmission occurs when there is no direct human-to-human contact. Contact occurs from a reservoir to contaminated surfaces or objects, or to vectors such as mosquitoes, flies, mites, fleas, ticks, rodents, or dogs. *dhss.delaware.gov/dph/files/directindtranspi.pdf*

Continuous Positive Airway Pressure (CPAP): a common treatment for obstructive sleep apnea. A CPAP machine uses a hose and mask or nosepiece to deliver constant and steady air pressure. *www.mayoclinic.org/diseases-conditions/sleep-apnea/in-depth/cpap/art-20044164*

Coronavirus Disease (COVID-19): an infectious disease caused by the SARS-CoV-2 virus. Most people infected with the virus will experience mild to moderate respiratory illness and recover without requiring special treatment. However, some will become seriously ill and require medical attention. Older people and those with underlying medical conditions like cardiovascular disease, diabetes, chronic respiratory disease, or cancer are more likely to develop serious illness. Anyone can get sick with COVID-19 and become seriously ill or die at any age.

Dead on Arrival (DOA): having died before getting to a hospital, emergency room, etc. *www.merriam-webster.com/dictionary/dead%20on%20arrival*

Dialysis: a treatment for kidney failure that rids one's body of unwanted toxins, waste products, and excess fluids by filtering the blood. *www.freseniuskidneycare.com/treatment/dialysis*

Directed Plan of Correction (DPOC): an enforcement remedy—just like a civil money penalty, or denial of payment. It identifies specific actions a facility must take in response to a deficiency, which may include policy and procedure changes, education of staff, and so on. CMS may impose a DPOC in combination with other remedies. *www.leadingagemn.org/news/mdh-addresses-questions-on-directed-plans-of-correction-to-nursing-homes*

Director of Nurses (DON): responsible to the owner/governing body/licensed administrator for the overall coordination and execution of nursing services, and monitoring and evaluating the outcomes of nursing care. *achca.memberclicks.net/assets/docs/ltcplc_core_func-r_6-07lw.pdf*

Doctors Without Borders/Médecins Sans Frontières (MSF): a vibrant movement made up of people from all corners of the world who share a common purpose: to save the lives and alleviate the suffering of people in danger by delivering medical care where it is needed most. *www.doctorswithoutborders.org/who-we-are/how-we-work/associations*

Droplet transmission: occurs by the direct spray of large droplets onto conjunctiva or mucous membranes of a susceptible host when an infected patient sneezes, talks, or coughs. *www.ncbi.nlm.nih.gov/pmc/articles/PMC7293495/*

Ebola: a virus that causes problems with how a person's blood clots. It is known as a hemorrhagic fever virus, because the clotting problems lead to internal bleeding, as blood leaks from small blood vessels in the body. The virus also causes inflammation and tissue damage. *www.hopkinsmedicine.org/ebola/about-the-ebola-virus.html*

Enterobacter: bacteria species are responsible for causing many nosocomial infections, and less commonly community-acquired infections, including urinary tract infections (UTI), respiratory infections, soft tissue infections, osteomyelitis, and endocarditis, among many others. *www.ncbi.nlm.nih.gov/books/NBK559296*

Environmental cleaning/services: a multifaceted intervention that involves cleaning and disinfection (when indicated) of the environment alongside other key program elements (e.g., leadership support, training, monitoring, and feedback mechanisms). *www.cdc.gov/hai/pdfs/resource-limited/environmental-cleaning-RLS-H.pdf*

Escherichia: bacteria found in the environment, foods, and intestines of people and animals. E. coli are a large and diverse group of bacteria. Although most strains of E. coli are harmless, others can make you sick. Some kinds of E. coli can cause diarrhea, while others cause urinary tract infections, respiratory illness and pneumonia, and other illnesses. *www.cdc.gov/ecoli/index.html*

Federal Emergency Management Agency (FEMA): The agency's mission is to support the "citizens and first responders ensuring that as a nation we work together to build, sustain, and improve our capability to prepare for, protect against, respond to, recover from, and mitigate all hazards." *doee.dc.gov/sites/default/files/dc/sites/ddoe/publication/attachments/Q-A_strormwater.pdf*

Fit testing: tests the seal between the N95 mask's, or respirator's, facepiece and your face. It typically takes fifteen to twenty minutes to complete and should be performed when this type of mask is first used and then at least annually. The purpose of the fit test is to assure that the mask fits and seals properly so potentially contaminated air cannot leak into the mask and so hazardous substances are kept out. *success.ada.org/~/media/CPS/Files/covid/Conducting_Respirator_Fit_Tests_And_Seal_Checks.pdf*

Five-Star Quality Rating System: CMS created the Five-Star Quality Rating System to help consumers, their families, and caregivers compare nursing homes more easily and to help identify areas about which you may want to ask questions. The Nursing Home Compare Web site features a quality rating system that gives each nursing home a rating of between one and five stars. Nursing homes with five stars are considered to have much above-average quality, and nursing homes with one star are considered to have quality much below average. There is one overall five-star rating for each nursing home, and a separate rating for each of the following three sources of information: health inspections, staffing, and quality measures. *www.cms.gov/Medicare/Provider-Enrollment-and-Certification/CertificationandComplianc/FSQRS*

Government Accountability Office (GAO): often called the "congressional watchdog," is an independent, non-partisan agency that works for Congress. GAO examines how taxpayer dollars are spent and provides Congress and federal agencies with objective, non-partisan, fact-based information to help the government save money and work more efficiently. *www.gao.gov/about*

Green zone: The zones (red, yellow, and green) refer to units or, in some cases, entire facilities. A unit is defined as an area of the facility where the staff are not typically shared with other areas during one shift. COVID-19 test negative, non-exposed. *www.chesco.org/DocumentCenter/View/55840/Cohorting-Strategies-for-covid-19_final-slides*

Healthcare-Associated Infections (HAI): infections people get while they're receiving healthcare for another condition. HAIs can happen in any healthcare facility, including hospitals, ambulatory surgical centers, end-stage renal disease facilities, and long-term care facilities. *health.gov/our-work/national-health-initiatives/health-care-quality/health-care-associated-infections*

Hepatitis B: a vaccine-preventable liver infection caused by the hepatitis B virus (HBV). Hepatitis B is spread when blood, semen, or other body fluids from a person infected with the virus enters the body of someone who is not infected. *www.cdc.gov/hepatitis/hbv/index.htm*

H1N1 flu (swine flu): primarily caused by the H1N1 strain of the flu (influenza) virus. H1N1 is a type of influenza A virus, and H1N1 is one of several flu virus strains that can cause the seasonal flu. Symptoms of the H1N1 flu are the same as those of the seasonal flu.

Hospital Health Improvement Innovation Network (HIIN): a national initiative to prevent patient harm and improve care in hospitals across the US. *cha.com/hospital-improvement-innovation-network-hiin*

Immediate Jeopardy: represents a situation in which entity non-compliance has placed the health and safety of recipients in its care at risk for serious injury, serious harm, serious impairment, or death.

These situations must be accurately identified by surveyors, thoroughly investigated, and resolved by the entity as quickly as possible. *www.cms.gov/Regulations-and-Guidance/Guidance/Manuals/downloads/som107ap_q_immedjeopardy.pdf*

Immunocompromised: having a weakened immune system. People who are immunocompromised have a reduced ability to fight infections and other diseases. This may be caused by certain diseases or conditions, such as AIDS, cancer, diabetes, malnutrition, and certain genetic disorders. It may also be caused by certain medicines or treatments, such as anticancer drugs, radiation therapy, and stem cell or organ transplant. Also called immunosuppressed. *www.cancer.gov/publications/dictionaries/cancer-terms/def/immunocompromised*

Independent living: Independent living is simply any housing arrangement designed exclusively for older adults, generally those aged fifty-five and over. Housing varies widely, from apartment-style living to single-family detached homes. In general, the housing is friendlier to aging adults, often being more compact, with easier navigation and no maintenance or yard work to worry about. Since independent living facilities are aimed at older adults who need little or no assistance with activities of daily living, most do not offer medical care or nursing staff. You can, however, hire in-home help separately as required. *www.helpguide.org/articles/senior-housing/independent-living-for-seniors.htm*

Infection Prevention and Control Program (IPCP): designed to provide a safe, sanitary, and comfortable environment and to help prevent the development and transmission of communicable diseases and infections. This program must include, at a minimum, a system for preventing, identifying, reporting, investigating, and controlling infections and communicable diseases for all residents, staff, and visitors. The IPCP must follow national standards and guidelines. *azdhs.gov/documents/preparedness/epidemiology-disease-control/healthcare-associated-infection/advisory-committee/long-term-care/cms-rule-toolkit.pdf*

Infection preventionist: an expert who helps to protect people from healthcare-associated infections. They work in many healthcare settings to keep patients, visitors, volunteers, employees, and healthcare providers safe from infection. *apic.org/Resource_/TinyMceFileManager/ip_and_You/IPandYou_SmallFlyer_download_hiq.pdf*

Influenza: a viral infection that attacks the respiratory system—the nose, throat and lungs. Influenza is commonly called the flu, but it's not the same as stomach "flu" viruses that cause diarrhea and vomiting. *www.mayoclinic.org/diseases-conditions/flu/symptoms-causes/syc-20351719*

Intensive Care Unit (ICU): an organized system for the provision of care to critically ill patients that provides intensive and specialized medical and nursing care, an enhanced capacity for monitoring, and multiple modalities of physiologic organ support to sustain life during a period of life-threatening organ system insufficiency. *pubmed.ncbi.nlm.nih.gov/27612678*

Instacart: a service that allows you to order groceries from local grocery stores through the Instacart website or app and have them delivered to your door in as little as two hours. *www.healthline.com/nutrition/how-does-instacart-work#_noHeaderPrefixedContent*

The Joint Commission (TJC): The mission of The Joint Commission is to continuously improve health care for the public, in collaboration with other stakeholders, by evaluating health care organizations and inspiring them to excel in providing safe and effective care of the highest quality and value. Its vision is that all people always experience the safest, highest quality, best-value health care across all settings. *www.jointcommission.org/about-us/*

K-N95: Chinese standard of respirator masks. *www.ancor.org/newsroom/news/n95-vs-kn95-masks-whats-difference*

Klebsiella: a type of Gram-negative bacteria that can cause different types of healthcare-associated infections, including pneumonia, bloodstream infections, wound or surgical site infections, and meningitis. *www.cdc.gov/hai/organisms/klebsiella/klebsiella.html*

Licensed Practical Nurse (LPN): a nurse that performs basic patient care tasks and helps to keep patients comfortable. LPNs work under the supervision of Registered Nurses (RNs) and other medical professionals. *nurse.org/resources/licensed-practical-nurse-lpn-lvn*

Long-Term Care Facility (LTCF): facilities providing a spectrum of medical and non-medical supports and services to frail or older adults unable to reside independently in the community. The following LTCFs are able to use NHSN for surveillance: nursing homes (NH) and skilled nursing facilities (SNF), intermediate/chronic care facilities for the developmentally disabled, and assisted living facilities and residential care facilities. *www.cdc.gov/nhsn/pdfs/ltc/ltcf-key-terms-acronyms_current.pdf*

Malaria: a serious and sometimes fatal disease caused by a parasite that commonly infects a certain type of mosquito which feeds on humans. People who get malaria are typically very sick with high fevers, shaking chills, and flu-like illness. *www.cdc.gov/malaria/about/faqs.html*

Maryland Department of Health, Office of Health Care Quality (OHCQ): the agency within the Maryland Department of Health charged with monitoring the quality of care in Maryland's healthcare facilities and community-based programs. *health.maryland.gov/ohcq/Pages/home.aspx*

McGeer Surveillance: standardized guidance for infection surveillance activities and research studies in nursing homes and similar institutions. *www.jstor.org/stable/10.1086/667743#metadata_info_tab_contents*

Measles: a highly contagious illness caused by a virus that replicates in the nose and throat of an infected child or adult. Then, when someone with measles coughs, sneezes or talks, infected droplets spray into the air, where other people can inhale them. The infected droplets may also land on a surface, where they remain active and contagious for several hours. You can contract the virus by putting your fingers in your mouth or nose or rubbing your eyes after touching the infected surface. About 90 percent of susceptible people who are exposed to someone with the virus will be infected. *www.mayoclinic.org/diseases-conditions/measles/symptoms-causes/syc-20374857*

Medicaid: A joint federal and state program that helps provide healthcare coverage for people with low incomes and limited resources. *www.cms.gov/Research-Statistics-Data-and-Systems/Research/ResearchGenInfo/Downloads/DataNav_Glossary_Alpha.pdf*

Medicare: Medicare is a health insurance program, administered by the United States government, for people who are aged sixty-five and over; to those who are under sixty-five and are permanently physically disabled or who have a congenital physical disability; or to those who meet other special criteria like the End Stage Renal Disease program (ESRD). *www.cms.gov/Research-Statistics-Data-and-Systems/Research/ResearchGenInfo/Downloads/DataNav_Glossary_Alpha.pdf*

Methicillin-resistant Staphylococcus aureus (MRSA): a cause of staph infection that is difficult to treat because of resistance to some antibiotics. *www.cdc.gov/mrsa/index.html*

Michigan Department of Health and Human Services (MDHHS): promotes better health outcomes, works to reduce health risks, and supports stable and safe families in Michigan while encouraging self-sufficiency. *www.linkedin.com/company/michigan-department-of-health-&-human-services*

Minimum Data Set (MDS): part of the federally mandated process for clinical assessment of all residents in Medicare and Medicaid-certified nursing homes. This process provides a comprehensive assessment of each resident's functional capabilities and helps nursing home staff identify health problems. *www.cms.gov/Research-Statistics-Data-and-Systems/Computer-Data-and-Systems/Minimum-Data-Set-3-0-Public-Reports*

Minimum Data Set (MDS) coordinator: responsible for gathering information on a healthcare facility's current and future patients for future assessment, including physical and mental states. MDS coordinators assess charts and communicate with healthcare teams to create applicable healthcare plans for their current and incoming residents. An MDS coordinator usually works in a nursing home or other healthcare facility. *www.glassdoor.com/Job-Descriptions/mds-Coordinator.htm*

Mucous membranes: The moist, inner lining of some organs and body cavities (such as the nose, mouth, lungs, and stomach). Glands in the mucous membrane make mucus (a thick, slippery fluid). Also called mucosa.

Multidrug-Resistant Organisms (MDROs): bacteria that have become resistant to certain antibiotics and can no longer be used to control or kill the bacteria. *portal.ct.gov/DPH/hai/MultidrugResistant-Organisms-MDROs-What-Are-They*

National Academy of Medicine's Institute of Medicine (IOM): one of three academies that make up the National Academies of Sciences, Engineering, and Medicine (the National Academies) in the United States. Operating under the 1863 Congressional charter of the National Academy of Sciences, the National Academies are private, nonprofit institutions that work outside of government to provide objective advice on matters of science, technology, and health. *nam.edu/about-the-nam/*

National Consumer Voice for Quality Long-Term Care: the leading national voice representing consumers in issues related to long-term care, helping to ensure that consumers are empowered to advocate for themselves. The Consumer Voice is a primary source of information and tools for consumers, families, caregivers, advocates, and ombudsmen to help ensure quality care for the individual. *theconsumervoice.org/about*

National Healthcare Safety Network (NHSN): the nation's most widely used healthcare-associated infection tracking system. NHSN provides facilities, states, regions, and the nation with data needed to identify problem areas, measure progress of prevention efforts, and ultimately eliminate healthcare-associated infections. *www.cdc.gov/nhsn/index.html*

National Institute of Health (NIH): a part of the US Department of Health and Human Services; the nation's medical research agency—making important discoveries that improve health and save lives. *www.nih.gov/about-nih/who-we-are*

Negative air pressure room: when the air pressure inside the room is lower than the air pressure outside the room. This means that when the door is opened, potentially contaminated air or other dangerous particles from inside the room will not flow outside into non-contaminated areas. *www.news-medical.net/health/What-are-Negative-Pressure-Rooms.aspx*

Non-governmental organization (NGO): an organization that undertakes a wide array of activities, including political advocacy on issues such as foreign policy, elections, the environment, healthcare, women's rights, economic development, and many other issues. They often develop and address new approaches to social and economic problems that governments cannot address alone. *www.state.gov/non-governmental-organizations-ngos-in-the-united-states/*

N95 Respirator: a respiratory protective device designed to achieve a very close facial fit and very efficient filtration of airborne particles. *www.fda.gov/medical-devices/personal-protective-equipment-infection-control/n95-respirators-surgical-masks-face-masks-and-barrier-face-coverings*

Nursing home: Nursing homes, also called skilled nursing facilities, provide a wide range of health and personal care services. Their services focus on medical care more than most assisted living facilities. These services typically include nursing care, twenty-four-hour supervision, three meals a day, and assistance with everyday activities. Rehabilitation services—such as physical, occupational, and speech therapy—are also available. Some people stay at a nursing home for a short time after being in the hospital. After they recover, they go home. However, most nursing home residents live there permanently because they have ongoing physical or mental conditions that require constant care and supervision. *www.nia.nih.gov/health/residential-facilities-assisted-living-and-nursing-homes*

Observational unit: a dedicated unit built to provide efficient protocol-based care to patients with well-defined diagnoses or presenting symptoms such as chest pain, asthma, and congestive heart failure. *link.springer.com/article/10.1007/s40138-013-0038-y*

Occupational Safety and Health Administration (OSHA): "With the Occupational Safety and Health Act of 1970, Congress created the Occupational Safety and Health Administration (OSHA) to ensure safe and healthful working conditions for workers by setting and enforcing standards and by providing training, outreach, education and assistance." *www.osha.gov/aboutosha*

Office of Disease Prevention and Health Promotion (ODPHP): plays a vital role in keeping the nation healthy. ODPHP accomplishes this by setting national public health objectives and supporting programs, services, and education activities that improve the health of all Americans. "Congress created ODPHP in 1976 to lead disease prevention and health promotion efforts in the United States. We're part of the US Department of Health and Human Services under the Office of the Assistant Secretary for Health." *health.gov/about-odphp*

Ombudsman: a citizen's representative. Ombudsmen help resolve problems related to the health, safety, welfare, and rights of nursing home residents. Each state has a long-term care (LTC) ombudsman program with thousands of ombudsmen to improve senior care at the local and national levels. Ombudsmen can be a part of paid staff or work on a volunteer basis. *www.nursinghomeabuse.org/nursing-home-abuse/ombudsman/*

Pandemic: occurring over a wide geographic area (such as multiple countries or continents) and typically affecting a significant proportion of the population. *www.merriam-webster.com/dictionary/pandemic*

Paraprofessional Healthcare Institute (PHI): works to ensure quality care for older adults and people with disabilities by creating quality jobs for direct care workers. *phinational.org/*

Patient Protection and Affordability Act: The law was amended by the Health Care and Education Reconciliation Act on March 30, 2010. The name "Affordable Care Act" is usually used to refer to the final, amended version of the law. (It's sometimes known as "PPACA," "ACA," or "Obamacare."). The law provides numerous rights and protections that make health coverage more fair and easy to understand, along with subsidies (through "premium tax credits" and "cost-sharing reductions") to make it more affordable. The law also expands the Medicaid program to cover more people with low incomes. *www.healthcare.gov/glossary/patient-protection-and-affordable-care-act/*

Pediatric/children's hospital: Children's hospitals play a central role in advancing the health of all children. From prevention to critical care, children's hospitals meet the healthcare needs of children twenty-four hours a day, 365 days a year. Working in and with communities, children's hospitals lead health improvement initiatives for children that yield long-term benefits, including a healthier adult population and workforce, and countless costs avoided by early intervention in—or even prevention of—chronic health problems. *www.childrenshospitals.org/about-us/about-childrens-hospitals*

Performance Improvement Projects (PIP): a concentrated effort on a particular problem in one area of the facility or facility wide; it involves gathering information systematically to clarify issues or problems, and intervening for improvements. *www.cms.gov/medicare/provider-enrollment-and-certification/qapi/downloads/qapiataglance.pdf*

Personal Protective Equipment (PPE): equipment worn to minimize exposure to hazards that cause serious workplace injuries and illnesses. These injuries and illnesses may result from contact with chemical, radiological, physical, electrical, mechanical, or other workplace hazards. Personal protective equipment may include items such as gloves, safety glasses and shoes, earplugs or muffs, hard hats, respirators, or coveralls, vests, and full body suits. *www.osha.gov/personal-protective-equipment*

Plan of Correction (POC): a plan developed by the facility and approved by CMS or the survey agency that describes the actions the facility will take to correct deficiencies and specifies the date by which those deficiencies will be corrected. *www.cms.gov/Medicare/Provider-Enrollment-and-Certification/SurveyCertificationEnforcement/Downloads/NH-Enforcement-FAQ.pdf*

Powered Air-Purifying Respirator (PAPR): an air-purifying respirator that uses a blower to force air through filter cartridges or canisters and into the breathing zone of the wearer. This process creates an air flow inside either a tight-fitting facepiece or loose-fitting hood or helmet, providing a higher assigned protection factor (APF) than the reusable elastomeric non-powered air-purifying half facepiece (half mask) or N95 FFRs. A PAPR can be used for protection during healthcare procedures in which HCP are exposed to greater risks of aerosolized pathogens causing acute respiratory infections. *www.cdc.gov/coronavirus/2019-ncov/hcp/ppe-strategy/powered-air-purifying-respirators-strategy.html*

Punitive: serving for, concerned with, or inflicting punishment. *www.dictionary.com/browse/punitive*

Quality Assurance (QA): the specification of standards for quality of service and outcomes, and a process throughout the organization for assuring that care is maintained at acceptable levels in relation to those standards. QA is ongoing, both anticipatory and retrospective in its efforts to identify how the organization is performing, including where and why facility performance is at risk or has failed to meet standards. *www.cms.gov/Medicare/Provider-Enrollment-and-Certification/QAPI/qapidefinition*

Quality Improvement (QI): the continuous study and improvement of processes with the intent to better services or outcomes, and prevent or decrease the likelihood of problems, by identifying areas of opportunity and testing new approaches to fix underlying causes of persistent/systemic problems or barriers to improvement. QI in nursing homes aims to improve processes involved in healthcare delivery and resident quality of life. QI can make good quality even better. *www.cms.gov/Medicare/Provider-Enrollment-and-Certification/QAPI/qapidefinition*

Quality measures: come from resident assessment data that nursing homes routinely collect on the residents at specified intervals during their stay. These measures assess the resident's physical and clinical conditions and abilities, as well as preferences and life care wishes. These assessment data have been converted to develop quality measures that give consumers another source of information that shows how well nursing homes are caring for their residents' physical and clinical needs. *www.cms.gov/Medicare/Quality-Initiatives-Patient-Assessment-Instruments/NursingHomeQualityInits/NHQIQualityMeasures*

Red zone: The zones (red, yellow, and green) refer to units or in some cases, entire facilities. A unit is defined as an area of the facility where the staff are not typically shared with other areas during one shift. COVID-19 test positive. *www.chesco.org/DocumentCenter/View/55840/Cohorting-Strategies-for-covid-19_final-slides*

Regulatory: of or relating to the control or direction of an activity by a set of rules, laws, etc. *www.dictionary.com/browse/regulatory*

Resident Assessment Instrument (RAI): helps nursing home staff in gathering definitive information on a resident's strengths and needs, which must be addressed in an individualized care plan. Interdisciplinary use of the RAI promotes this emphasis on quality of care and quality of life. *www.aapacn.org/resources/rai-manual/*

Salmonellosis: an infection with a bacteria called Salmonella. Salmonella live in the intestinal tracts of animals, including birds. Salmonella are usually transmitted to humans by eating foods contaminated with animal feces. *www.health.state.mn.us/diseases/salmonellosis/basics.html*

Scabies: an itchy skin condition caused by a tiny burrowing mite called Sarcoptes scabiei. Intense itching occurs in the area where the mite burrows. The urge to scratch may be especially strong at night. Scabies is contagious and can spread quickly through close physical contact in a family, childcare group, school class, nursing home or prison. Because scabies is so contagious, doctors often recommend treatment for entire families or contact groups. *www.mayoclinic.org/diseases-conditions/scabies/symptoms-causes/syc-20377378*

Secure Access Management Services (SAMS): The Centers for Disease Control and Prevention's (CDC) Secure Access Management Services

(SAMS) is a federal information technology (IT) system that gives authorized personnel secure access to non-public CDC applications. The SAMS partner portal is a website designed to provide centralized access to public health information and computer applications operated by the CDC. For the National Healthcare Safety Network (NHSN) Program, SAMS will provide healthcare facilities and other partners, such as state health departments and QIOs, with secure and immediate access to the NHSN application. *www.cdc.gov/nhsn/sams/about-sams.html*

Sepsis: a potentially life-threatening condition that occurs when the body's response to an infection damages its own tissues. When the infection-fighting processes turn on the body, they cause organs to function poorly and abnormally. Sepsis may progress to septic shock. This is a dramatic drop in blood pressure that can lead to severe organ problems and death. Early treatment with antibiotics and intravenous fluids improves chances for survival. *www.mayoclinic.org/diseases-conditions/sepsis/symptoms-causes/syc-20351214*

Severe Acute Respiratory Syndrome (SARS): a respiratory illness that affected many people worldwide in 2003. It was caused by a coronavirus, called SARS-associated coronavirus (SARS-COV-2). SARS was first reported in Asia in February 2003. The illness spread to twenty-nine countries, where 8,096 people got SARS and 774 of them died. The SARS global outbreak was contained in July 2003. Since 2004, there have not been any known cases of SARS reported anywhere in the world. *www.cdc.gov/dotw/sars/index.html*

Shigella: bacteria that cause an infection called shigellosis. Most people with Shigella infection have diarrhea (sometimes bloody), fever, and stomach cramps. Symptoms usually begin one to two days after infection and last seven days. Most people recover without needing antibiotics. However, people with severe illness and those with underlying conditions that weaken the immune system should be given antibiotics. Antibiotics can shorten the duration of illness (by about two days) and might help reduce the spread of Shigella to others. *www.cdc.gov/shigella/index.html*

Skilled Nursing Facility (SNF): a facility engaged primarily in providing skilled nursing care and rehabilitation services for residents who require such care because of injury, disability, or illness. A large percentage of SNFs are dually certified as both SNFs and nursing homes. *www.cdc.gov/nhsn/pdfs/ltc/ltcf-key-terms-acronyms_current.pdf*

Small Volume Nebulizer (SVN): an aerosol generator used to deliver liquid medications (e.g., bronchodilators) to the mid-to-lower airways. High velocity pressurized airflow is used to convert drug solutions into fine mists with particles that can then be inhaled using a facemask or mouthpiece. *www.aarc.org/wp-content/uploads/2014/08/aerosol_guide_pro.pdf*

Statewide Program for Infection Control and Epidemiology (SPICE): promotes prevention and control of healthcare-associated infections in North Carolina and beyond by providing evidence-based education and consultation across the healthcare spectrum. *spice.unc.edu/about/*

Statistical Analysis Software (SAS): a command-driven statistical software suite widely used for statistical data analysis and visualization. It allows one to use qualitative techniques and processes which help to enhance employee productivity and business profits. *www.guru99.com/sas-tutorial.html*

Transmission-based precautions: the second tier of basic infection control and are to be used in addition to Standard Precautions for patients who may be infected or colonized with certain infectious agents for which additional precautions are needed to prevent infection transmission. *www.cdc.gov/infectioncontrol/basics/transmission-based-precautions.html*

Tuberculosis (TB): caused by a bacterium called Mycobacterium tuberculosis. The bacteria usually attack the lungs, but TB bacteria can attack any part of the body such as the kidney, spine, and brain. Not everyone infected with TB bacteria becomes sick. As a result, two TB-related conditions exist: latent TB infection (LTBI) and TB disease. If not treated properly, TB disease can be fatal. *www.cdc.gov/tb/topic/basics/default.htm*

United States Senate Special Committee on Aging: Throughout its existence, the Special Committee on Aging has served as a focal point in the Senate for discussion and debate on matters relating to older Americans. Often, the Committee will submit its findings and recommendations for legislation to the Senate. In addition, the Committee publishes materials of assistance to those interested in public policies which relate to the elderly. *www.aging.senate.gov/about/history*

Urinary Tract Infections (UTIs): infections in any part of a person's urinary system—the kidneys, ureters, bladder, and urethra. Most infections involve the lower urinary tract—the bladder and the urethra. *www.mayoclinic.org/diseases-conditions/urinary-tract-infection/symptoms-causes/syc-20353447*

US Department of Health and Human Services (HHS): The mission of the US Department of Health and Human Services (HHS) is to enhance the health and well-being of all Americans, by providing for effective health and human services and by fostering sound, sustained advances in the sciences underlying medicine, public health, and social services. *www.hhs.gov/about/index.html*

Whooping cough: a highly contagious respiratory tract infection. In many people, it's marked by a severe hacking cough followed by a high-pitched intake of breath that sounds like "whoop." Before the vaccine was developed, whooping cough was considered a childhood disease. Now whooping cough primarily affects children too young to have completed the full course of vaccinations and teenagers and adults whose immunity has faded. Deaths associated with whooping cough are rare but most commonly occur in infants. That's why it's so important for pregnant women—and other people who will have close contact with an infant—to be vaccinated against whooping cough. *www.mayoclinic.org/diseases-conditions/whooping-cough/symptoms-causes/syc-20378973*

Yellow zone: The zones (red, yellow, and green) refer to units or in some cases, entire facilities. A unit is defined as an area of the facility where the staff are not typically shared with other areas during one shift. COVID-19 test negative, but resident is within fourteen days of exposure. *www.chesco.org/DocumentCenter/View/55840/Cohorting-Strategies-for-covid-19_final-slides*

Yersinia: an infection caused most often by eating raw or undercooked pork contaminated with Yersinia enterocolitica bacteria. CDC estimates Y. enterocolitica causes almost 117,000 illnesses, 640 hospitalizations, and 35 deaths in the United States every year. Children are infected more often than adults, and the infection is more common in the winter. *www.cdc.gov/yersinia/index.html*